Ask the Bishop

"Bishop Monforton provides for us a whimsical and down-to-earth apologetic with regard to the mysteries of the Catholic faith. The reader will greatly enjoy his responses to the questions of children."

MOST REV. MICHAEL BYRNES
Archbishop of Agaña

"Rare is the bishop who is willing to answer the questions of his people—and is able to answer in the language of their hearts. Such a man is Bishop Jeffrey Monforton. I pray that this book will amplify his voice well beyond his 'little flock,' of which I'm pleased to be a member."

SCOTT HAHN
Founder and President, the St. Paul Center

"Bishop Monforton's *Ask the Bishop* is a wonderful example of how our faith seeks understanding through questions. He uses this format as an opportunity to teach and catechize. Bishop Monforton's answers are authentic and practical. He extends himself as our shepherd, wishing only to bring us closer to Christ through a great understanding of our faith. *Ask the Bishop* is a great resource for all ages!"

THOMAS J. COSTELLO
Principal, Catholic Central High School, Steubenville, Ohio

Ask the Bishop

QUESTIONS AND ANSWERS OVER THE YEARS

BISHOP JEFFREY M. MONFORTON

EMMAUS ROAD
PUBLISHING

Steubenville, Ohio
www.emmausroad.org

Emmaus Road Publishing
1468 Parkview Circle
Steubenville, Ohio 43952

Library of Congress Control Number: 2020938969
ISBN: 978-1-949013-99-3 (pb)

Cover design and layout by Emily Demary
Cover image: *St Thomas of Villanueva* (17th century)
by Francisco Camilo, Museo del Prado, Madrid, Spain

To my parents, Marc and Virginia Monforton
My first teachers of the Catholic Faith

I would like to acknowledge the Office of Christian Formation and Schools, the St. Paul Center, Emmaus Road Publishing & Emmaus Academic, and the Youth of the Diocese of Steubenville.

TABLE OF CONTENTS

INTRODUCTION

IN MY FIRST THEOLOGY CLASS as a seminarian, I discovered the meaning of theology in the words of St. Anselm of Canterbury: *faith seeking understanding.* These words have stood the test of time for more than ten centuries. This former Bishop of Canterbury underscored the fact that faith and reason are not hugely exclusive; one depends on the other.

This corollary has helped craft my service of walking in the footsteps of the Good Shepherd since my early days as a priest. In my first assignment at the Shrine of the Little Flower (now the National Shrine of the Little Flower Basilica), I would engage in impromptu "Ask the Priest" sessions, which gave students the opportunity to ask questions about their faith, or, as one may conclude, to allow them to participate in "stump the priest." Most certainly with wisdom comes humility. This adherence to the formal or informal setting of "Ask the Priest" accompanied me through my parish assignments and parish or school visits. It seems to me that regardless of the maturity of one's faith, if a person is willing to ask questions about his or her faith, then their faith matters to them, even in the slightest. I believe that I have an obligation to answer those questions about our faith, even when there are times that my first answer is "I need to research this before offering a complete answer."

As I approach the twenty-sixth anniversary of my priestly ordination this June, I am honored to share this anniversary with the inception of "Ask the Priest," which has now developed into "Ask the Bishop" with my episcopal ordination in 2012.

Following my episcopal ordination, it was harder for me to offer impromptu question and answer sessions, so I chose a more formal route by publishing three "Ask the Bishop" questions each month in the diocesan newspaper, *The Steubenville Register*. While the sources of each one of these questions were our own Catholic school students, kindergarten through twelfth grade, I quickly realized in visits with parishioners throughout the diocese that it was primarily the adults who read the "Ask the Bishop" section of the paper. The questions also are published on the diocesan website.

With respect to his apostolic office, the bishop is a herald of the Gospel. A herald's vocabulary does not stand on its own with "because I told you so." In an era of secular relativism, accompanied by so many people equating religion with superstition, an apologetic attitude is essential. This book by no means is intended to replace any ecclesiastical publication, most certainly not the Catechism of the Catholic Church, but it is my hope that *Ask the Bishop* may further assist the reader in better understanding our Catholic faith and the purpose behind why we do certain things as believers. I am grateful to Emmaus Road Publishing for agreeing to publish this work as each one of us joyfully shares with others our daily encounter with Jesus Christ.

May you and I be willing to invite and answer all thoughtful questions about our faith with all whom we encounter. May God bless you on your Christian sojourn deepening your understanding of our faith in Our Lord and Savior Jesus Christ. Immaculate Heart of Mary, patroness of the Diocese of Steubenville, *pray for us.*

Fides Quaerens Intellectum

CREED

Why do you believe in God?

That is a question that has been asked throughout the ages. We know that faith is a gift from God. And that very gift of God is meant to be nurtured in our lives, especially through prayer and the reception of the sacraments.

From the moment I was very small I believed in God, but it was necessary for my faith in God to grow. Moreover, my love for Jesus deepened as I continued to progress in my knowledge that Jesus is always with me and has given his life for me in order that I may be one with him.

I believe in God because I lovingly respond to God's invitation to believe in him. There is nothing magical about this, for it is completely real. I love God dearly and I wish to learn more about him each and every day, and I do so by doing my very best, through God's grace, to imitate him. My belief in God is not governed by "have to," but instead, "I want to." Jesus invites, and I respond.

We all are aware of our family members and friends who possess varying degrees of faith, from what may seem to be very little to an extraordinary amount. I believe in God, of course, as he has invited me into his life, and I respond with inviting God into mine.

As you and I have learned from our relationships with family and friends, we want to have faith in them as well. And at times, it takes much work to foster or grow those relationships. In the end it is that love and friendship that governs our belief in one another and, most importantly, our belief in God. As we read in the Gospel according to John, "God so loved the world that he gave his only Son" (Jn 3:16).

How can you and I not wish to learn more about our best friend, Jesus, who gave his entire life in order that you and I may spend all eternity with him? I believe in God because I love God. I believe in God because I want to learn more about God. I believe in God because God wants me to dwell with him forever, and it begins with you and me allowing God into our lives now.

How do you prove to a realist that God is real?

This is a very timely question, for we live in an era where secularism has become a religion to some. Even worse, secular relativism has compromised the very fabric of our culture. However, before I get further onto my preaching pedestal, I will designate that subject to another time.

What I have done is set the stage, recognizing that we live in a world where people have lost or at the very least dampened their belief in a loving God. In your question, I suspect you are referring mostly to atheists, as well as agnostics—those who either believe there is no God or believe in a disinterested God who cares little about our destiny. As Christians, we recognize the fact that God created the world and that Jesus Christ, Son of God the Father, came to us and, as a result, suffered, died, and rose from the dead for you and for me. In other words, God does care.

As one who enjoyed science as a youth, I am edified to see the workings of God, especially through our scientific knowledge. We have among us priests and religious who, prior to entering the convent, friary, monastery, or seminary, worked in scientific fields such as in medicine, astrophysics, and engineering. When these individuals recognized their sacred vocation, they did not simply devalue or renounce their scientific background, but actually have fortified the Church with the appreciation of the created world.

You ask how we may prove to a realist that God is real. While faith is the beginning of our spiritual pilgrimage, some people may possess little or no faith in the living God. Loving compassion (and not pity) should rule our response to their inquiry about God. Perhaps we can begin by referring to certain stories in the Bible, beginning with the Good News of Jesus and his love for us. The Bible is more than a story about us. The Bible is the living Word of God. We encounter God. You may ask the person what keeps them from believing in God or, better yet, you may live your faith for all to see. Not in a boastful way, but live in a manner that others see you would like to share the Good News, while respecting where others may be in their journey here on Earth. As Pope Francis mentions time and time again, our encounter with others must begin with compassion and mercy.

We all are invited to be realists, for the reality is Jesus Christ is the same yesterday, today, and forever. The reality is God so loved the world that he sent us his only Son. God loves us more than you and I can imagine. As we quickly approach Holy Week and the sacred Easter Triduum, may we keep our eyes fixed on Jesus in our common Lenten pilgrimage.

How did God come to be?

God is eternal. In other words, God is the One who does the creating. The Book of Genesis instructs us that God created time and the universe in which we live. Of course, as people who measure what we do by "keeping time," it can be difficult to understand the concept that God has always been around.

Perhaps we may look at it this way: God created time for our benefit. God created the world in order that you and I may worship him and to share in his joy. God did not need us when he created us, but he certainly intended you and me to be here. Just as God's work is not limited to finite laws of this world, he is not limited by time, since he created it.

Speaking of time, people have been asking this question for a very long time. The Catechism of the Catholic Church even acknowledges this in paragraphs 282–285. As we ascertain the inner workings of the universe, such as through the laws of physics (as we understand them), more questions seem to emerge. In our common curiosity about the beginnings of creation, the understanding of an eternal God transcends the discipline of the external sciences.

God is. Whether or not we employ external scientific data or the Creation Narrative from the Book of Genesis, we account that God existed before time itself. The Catechism explains that "The existence of God the Creator can be known with certainty through his works, by the light of human reason" (286). Remember, "the created" is trying to understand the Creator. Not an easy task, but one that requires both faith and reason.

I bring up faith because we know God did not simply create the universe and walk away. That's called Deism, and it misses the point of Jesus' Suffering, death, and Resurrection: the New Creation. Only the One who existed before time could recreate the world in the divine gift of his Son. God is constantly with us and has willed the universe into existence, and recreated it in his Son for our benefit and for us in return to love God and to give him glory in our lives. God has no beginning, but out of his divine love, we do.

How is God three people in one person?

First of all, we should look at the words used to describe the Holy Trinity: *three persons, one God*. The faith life of every Christian is based on the reality of God the Father, God the Son, and God the Holy Spirit. Jesus himself revealed this truth in his prayer to his Father and in his teachings to his Apostles. To be Christian is to believe in and to be baptized in the "name of the Father and of the Son and of the Holy Spirit" (Mt 28:19).

Also, the Holy Trinity is a mystery that we profess as a truth in the Creed every Sunday. Many a book or article has been published concerning this mystery. It is our faith, which complements our ability to reason, that allows us to appreciate this truth. The Holy Trinity is an object of faith.

It seems easier to explain what the Holy Trinity is *not*. For instance, there are many components to a computer. Only when all the parts are put together do we have a computer. The screen itself is not a computer. Or, for those of us who know the periodic table from our days in school: When we combine two hydrogen atoms with one oxygen atom, we get water. There are three parts to water. Only when you combine them do you have water. While these examples give us some good images, neither is an accurate explanation of the Holy Trinity.

All three Persons of the Holy Trinity possess the fullness of God. This is very difficult for us human beings to comprehend with our limited reasoning ability. It requires faith in the words of Jesus to understand that God's plan for us greatly exceeds our human intellect.

If God knows what will happen to us after we die, does that mean we lack free will because we can't do anything to change what is already determined?

This is a question that many have struggled with when it comes to the truth behind our free will. We must remember that God is the master of all reality. The Catechism of the Catholic Church is quite clear when it states, ". . . the ways of his providence are often unknown to us. Only at the end, when our partial knowledge ceases, when we see God 'face to face,' will we fully know the ways by which . . . God has guided his creation to that definitive sabbath rest for which he created heaven and earth" (314).

While we are limited in our human nature to understand completely God's divine providence, we appreciate the fact that at the same time God has given us free will by which we journey to our ultimate destiny by our free choice and preferential love. We are not possessors of artificial intelligence, but instead real intelligence. God has given us the gift of free will, which makes us responsible for our own acts in that they are voluntary. Although God knows all things, he has entitled us with the ability to make our own choices.

God does not set us up for failure, but instead gives us the freedom to set ourselves up for failure . . . or for success, if we follow his will.

Why didn't God send Jesus earlier, like after Noah?

I guess I can be funny and say that God the Father did, in fact, send Jesus after Noah, but I believe you mean "right after" Noah. What that means in our salvation history is that God restored our friendship with him in the person of Jesus. With original sin, Adam and Eve destroyed our bond with God and, therefore, we lost our "grace of original holiness" (CCC 375). That holiness needed to be restored.

In God's divine wisdom, we have the very unfolding of salvation history. Just as we know that God created time, we also know that through his constant presence he had an overarching plan for humanity from the Old Testament times all the way to the conception and birth of Jesus.

The simple answer is, only God knows why his timing is perfect. The Old Testament times may have needed to happen to prepare God's people for the coming of Jesus as Messiah. For example, if Isaiah hadn't told us about the Suffering Servant (Is 52–53), it would be much harder to understand Jesus and his suffering on the Cross. Through the events of salvation history, God communicated truths that paved the way for the coming of Christ.

Why did God make carnivores if his commandment is thou shall not kill?

As we are referring to Exodus 20:2–17, it is good for us to take a look at the underlying meaning of all the Ten Commandments. The Ten Commandments, also known as the Decalogue (or "ten words"), are instructions from God to be followed if we wish to be faithful to him. These laws were given to Moses a long time ago on Mount Sinai.

While each one of these laws is meant for us human beings, we must understand that these divine laws focus squarely on our relationship with one another. In other words, God is not ordering us to become vegetarians, but instead to make sure we respect the life of one another. Each one of us has been made in God's image and likeness and God does not want us to forget that. "Thou shall not kill" means for you and me to respect the life of one another as God has made us to be good. More simply, the commandment not to kill only applies to humans not killing other humans. We aren't supposed to kill because we are supposed to be like God. We live all of these commandments in light of the two commandments Jesus reminds us of as we are meant to love God and neighbor. It seems to me that those two commandments are the ones so many people find difficult to follow.

Why did God create animals?

In the Book of Genesis, we read that God created animals, and he called his creations good (see Gn 1:20–25). We also read that God entrusted the care of animals to us, and as we care for creation this includes respecting the interests of God's creatures. The animals are here for us, and we are their caretakers.

In his 2015 encyclical letter "Laudato Si'," Pope Francis instructs us that the care for our common home is both a moral and a spiritual challenge. In other words, the horizontal relationship between humanity and creation affects the vertical relationship between God and humanity: a call to inner conversion and personal transformation.

St. Francis of Assisi is a perfect example how we care for the animals entrusted us. Sometimes we may wonder why we have mosquitoes. But we should marvel at the mystery of creation, and that includes all species—including the new ones we continually discover.

Why did God create the knowledge tree if he knew they would eventually eat from it?

"You may freely eat of every tree in the garden, but of the tree of knowledge of good and evil you shall not eat, for in the day that you eat of it you shall die" (Gen 2:16–17). One would think that God telling Adam to avoid the tree would be sufficient reason to avoid the tree. As you point out, Adam and Eve failed to listen. They failed the test.

From the beginning, we human beings have been gifted with free choice; namely, to choose right from wrong. This story in the Book of Genesis is our beginning. From the very beginning, God has given us choices to follow him, or not (which is sin). Adam and Eve believed that the tree to which you refer was the solution to no longer being dependent on God. In other words, they chose to reject God.

Of course, God knows everything. We do not. Through the freely chosen rejection of God's instruction, original sin was introduced into the world. The story of Adam and Eve eating from the tree reminds us that because of original sin, we no longer enjoy the same relationship with God as they did in the beginning—until Jesus' Suffering, death, and Resurrection returned to us the grace lost at the origins of humanity.

The tree of knowledge is not the end of the story. Jesus restored us to our original state of grace through his Passion, death, and Resurrection. The Sacrament of Baptism is the eternal solution to the disobedience of our first parents. Adam and Eve failed miserably the test to avoid the tree, but Jesus has succeeded in returning us to grace.

How did God create our universe?

Before I proceed in answering this question, I recommend that you read the 1994 publication of "The Interpretation of the Bible in the Church" by the Pontifical Biblical Commission. This document is very helpful in delving into Sacred Scripture from the Book of Genesis to the Book of Revelation.

We learn from the Book of Genesis that God alone created the universe out of nothing. God's work was a loving act in the universe and for all of humanity. In the Catechism of the Catholic Church (beginning with paragraph 290), we are instructed that the creation of the universe is the work of the Holy Trinity. The eternal God gave the beginning to all that exists outside of himself, for he alone is the Creator.

While your question may have been focused on a visible description, which is presently debated among many in the scientific community, what is most important is for us to recognize who the source of the universe is and why God created the universe in the first place. As the Catechism explains further: "The world was created for the glory of God" (CCC 293). In other words, our universe is not a result of an accident but a deliberate act of love.

What is God doing while we are down here on Earth?

God is with you and me at this very moment. He wants us to hear his voice and to recognize his loving presence. For instance, when you participate in the sacraments, you encounter God. In the Eucharist, you receive the Body and Blood of Jesus. In the Sacrament of Penance, you speak directly to Jesus who is present in the person of the priest. Some may think that after God created the world he sat back, sort of like a clockmaker who builds a clock, sets the time, and sits back to watch it perform the measurement of time. Unlike the clockmaker, God is constantly involved in your life and mine. We just need to employ that keen eye of faith in order to recognize God's presence among us.

Jesus teaches us that we should recognize him in our neighbor, and we should treat others as we would treat Jesus. God has entrusted us with each other and has given each one of us a vocation in order to carry out his mission. The Church is the Body of Christ. Jesus has set us on a mission to share the Gospel, and we are to reach out to our neighbors in order that they may recognize God's presence among us. God's work is us. He leads us and remains with us in every situation and person we encounter.

We, also, are very aware that God does not watch us from a distance. He is very near to us, no matter where we find ourselves. Remember, Jesus tells us that he will never leave us. How greatly blessed we are to be deeply loved and treasured by God.

Why wasn't God down on Earth with Jesus?

Jesus is the Son of God, and as we read in the Gospel according to John, "The Word became flesh and dwelt among us" (Jn 1:14). Or, in another part of the Nativity story of Jesus where Joseph, in the midst of a dream, is informed by an angel that he will have a foster son and he will name him Emmanuel, which means "God is with us" (see Mt 20–25).

We also know that there are three persons and one God: God the Father, God the Son, and God the Holy Spirit. And, God the Father was with his Son Jesus all the time.

I apologize if this answer has all of a sudden become somewhat confusing, but that can happen when we explore the mysteries of our faith.

In other words, God was with Jesus all along as Jesus exercised his ministry of salvation here on Earth because Jesus is God. Just as God the Father never left Jesus even when Jesus was on the Cross, he will never leave us.

Why do we worship God?

The First Commandment in the Decalogue (the Ten Commandments) is quite clear about who deserves all of our worship, and only he, namely, God. Furthermore, as we hear time and time again: "God is love" (1 Jn 4:8). Out of that very love, God created us in his own image, and when our first parents betrayed him and brought original sin into the world, Jesus Christ was God's loving response for our salvation. But we worship God not simply because he created us; no, it goes much deeper than that.

Jesus' very words in the Lord's Prayer instruct us that we worship God alone, and that, in fact, he listens to our prayers. God has given you and me each a role in his plan for our salvation. Remember how Jesus responded to a question about what the most important commandment is: the first is that we should love God, and the second is that we are to love our neighbor as ourselves.

God is the source of all the good gifts in our lives, from family to anything with which we have been blessed. When we choose to worship God alone we freely accept the gifts of faith, hope, and love. As Christians we are called to place all of our faith in God, which means we acknowledge his divine authority. We place all of our hope in God for his limitless goodness and mercy. And, finally, we love God for all the treasures he has bestowed upon us, especially in the sacraments, as God's divine life is dispensed to us. God remains with us. We respond to his compassionate love and mercy in our daily worship.

In the Bible—Genesis 3:8—it says, "When they heard the sound of the Lord walking about the garden." My question is, back then, could God walk the earth like a human?

Often we might try to visualize what God looked like in the Book of Genesis. Adam and Eve had a privileged relationship with God because he created them in his own image and likeness and they were the first human beings created. You and I did not have the privilege to see the Garden of Eden before that most tragic act of disobedience by both Adam and Eve, so we are limited in our ability to see the Garden other than through the description in the Book of Genesis. God, being God, could appear to Adam and Eve in any manner he wished, and we know God spoke to Adam and Eve.

While it seems we have angels appearing in human form in the Book of Genesis, you and I can only imagine the form God took before Adam and Eve was certainly beautiful to behold.

Why does God sound so stern in the Old Testament, but Jesus is so kind, loving, and caring?

Many who are familiar with the Old Testament stories from the Book of Genesis through the prophets, prior to the birth of John the Baptist, recognize that time and time again God reprimanded his people for their transgressions. It seems that just when the people began to follow Our Lord, a distraction came, such as trying to replace God with idols.

Sometimes parents have to discipline their children to help them grow into the best version of themselves. This discipline doesn't mean parents don't love their children, even though it may feel like parents are being unkind in the moment. In the same way, God was consistently kind, loving, and caring to his people, even if they did not always recognize it.

However, with the birth of Jesus and subsequently his early mission, we witness in him God's enduring kindness, charity, and mercy. In other words, Jesus exemplifies all the goodness of God, for he is the Son of God.

You are correct in recognizing Jesus as kind, loving, and caring from all the stories we have heard or read in the Gospels and all of the New Testament books. The goodness and kindness that God the Father exercised in the Old Testament, even at times when he had to be quite stern with the chosen people as well as non-believers, comes to fruition in the person of Jesus. How blessed we are that God is so kind, loving, and caring!

If we are designed in God's image, then why do we still continue to sin?

This is a very good question in that one would think that if we are made in God's image and likeness we are incapable of any transgression. However, the Catechism of the Catholic Church instructs us that "Being in the image of God the human individual possesses the dignity of a person, who is not just something, but someone. He is capable of self-knowledge, of self-possession and of freely giving himself and entering into communion with other persons. And he is called by grace to a covenant with his Creator, to offer him a response of faith and love that no other creature can give in his stead" (CCC 357).

We should underline the word "freely" here. In other words, besides these enduring and magnificent gifts the Lord has given to each member of the human race, we have, in addition to those gifts, "free will."

Our first parents, Adam and Eve, demonstrated to us that we are created to be in communion with God, and when we break that relationship, we sin. You and I freely choose to follow God, and that requires docility of faith, as evidenced by Mary, the Mother of God.

Mary is proof positive that through the grace of God we possess the capacity to follow him unreservedly.

We, of course, have enough evidence from historical figures throughout human history that we also possess the capacity to turn away from God. Together, let us pray for an open heart to receive God's grace in order that we may freely serve him and imitate the members of the communion of saints.

If God created us to reflect who he is and he knows all and sees all, why does he let bad things happen?

You rightly say that we are made in God's image, as the Book of Genesis instructs. However, we also learn from the Bible that as we are given free will, we can misuse that very gift of free will to do ungodly things. We know that God created the world to be good. Unfortunately, our first parents, Adam and Eve, freely chose to sin in following their own will and not God's will. The damages done by original sin are evident in the world in the bad things people do.

While we have been saved through the Suffering, death,

Resurrection, and Ascension (Paschal Mystery) of Jesus, God continues to give us that gift of free will. Bad things happening in this world are a constant reminder that even though we are not yet in heaven, we have a responsibility to bring heaven here to Earth. The Sacrament of Baptism destroys original sin and gives us the opportunity to make the world a better place, as it was intended "in the beginning" (Gen 1:1).

Think about it this way: as our parents helped us to learn to walk or to ride a bike, there were times in that learning process we fell. Each time we were picked back up in order to try again. While we continue to make bad decisions from time to time, we can be confident that God will never leave us. He will remain with us always, to pick us up when we fall, for that is what a loving parent does. Our faith teaches us that sometime in the future Jesus will return to bring salvation history to a close and welcome us into heaven. In the meantime, may we not just recognize that God remains with us, but that through us he reaches out to victims of wrongdoing in the world. We are not "innocent bystanders" when we fail to address injustice—God calls us to help all those in need.

Do you think that God created us for a special reason or were we just what came to mind?

We read in the Book of Genesis that we were made in God's image and likeness (see Gen 1:26). In other words, you and I were not created because God had some leisure time and thought this would be a good idea. This is not to say, of course, that creating us was not a good idea, but for you to remember that God intentionally made you, me, and everyone.

That brings me to an important and related point: none of us is a mistake, nor is anybody unintended by God. Unfortunately, you and I live in a society where people have been encouraged to believe that their children could be unintended and a mistake. Thank goodness God does not think this way. Don't ever believe that your existence is a mistake—that belief is contrary to God's love and mercy.

God created us so that you and I may be loved by him. God did not need us, but at the same time, intended us. Think about how fortunate we are at this time to recognize God has created you and me and has intended us to be here to share his presence and love with so many of our fellow friends and neighbors, especially those who at this time believe that their lives are hopeless. By recognizing the truth that God intended us, you and I realize that no life is hopeless.

Not all members of our Church are living among us at this time. Those who have died have kept their citizenship in heaven. As a result, isn't it great to know that someday, at a time when God determines, we as a human family can be together with God celebrating the truth that he intended to create you and me and we are together as a family. The birth of Jesus at Christmas is a ringing reminder that God, from the beginning, intended to save all the human beings he created. One does not go to such extremes as sending his only Son among us to suffer and die for us so that we may go to heaven if we happen to simply be a good idea at the time. We are better than that, for God created us in his image and likeness.

Why did Jesus have to get baptized?

The short answer is: Jesus did it for us. Jesus, who is fully human and fully divine, wants us to be members of his family. In other words, through Jesus' baptism in the Jordan, we receive the Sacrament of Baptism. This is the first sacrament we all receive as Christians and is the first of three Sacraments of Initiation: Baptism, Eucharist, and Confirmation.

Jesus did not need to be baptized in the Jordan, but we needed him to be baptized in the Jordan in order to have the Sacrament of Baptism.

At his baptism, Jesus' true identity is acknowledged by God the Father and God the Holy Spirit. Here we have the Holy Trinity evident in this Gospel scene.

Jesus shows us that he is the author and source of all seven sacraments we have in the Catholic Church. There are immeasurable supernatural gifts which greatly exceed anything you and I can create.

What was Jesus' last name?

When Jesus was born, over 2,000 years ago, last names were uncommon. In ancient times there was little need for a last name. The name of one's father would be one way to describe a person, such as when James and John are named as "sons of Zebedee" in Mark 10:35. Jesus would have been known in reference to his foster father Joseph and his Mother Mary. A location also described a person, like "Jesus of Nazareth" (Mk 10:47). While you and I find it very helpful, even an honor to possess a last name, Jesus requires no last name. Jesus is the Son of God. The word *Christ* is a title that describes Jesus as the Messiah.

On the theme of titles, may you and I be ever grateful for our title of *Christian*. Our very identity has been personally given to us by Jesus himself, true God and true man. Jesus himself has made it possible for you and me to participate in the eternal gift of heaven with the Holy Trinity.

How did God die?

The short answer to your question is that God the Son died on the Cross on Mount Calvary. In the Passion narrative, we witness firsthand Jesus' human nature, as he offered up his life for our salvation. Furthermore, we recognize that following Jesus' death he rose from the dead, offering promise to all of us.

Each one of us should be profoundly grateful that God the Father so loved the world that he sent us his only Son for our salvation. And, in order for us to be redeemed, God the Son offered his life for us on the Cross. The next time you and I look at the crucifix, we should be thankful that Jesus Christ, the Son of God, gave up everything so that you and I might have eternal life.

As we ponder this mystery, may we all have renewed hope in the God who loves us more than you and I can fathom.

What year was Christ born, because we hear different years?

Good question, since you and I live in an era where we expect precision no matter what the subject. When there is no precision we become anxious and confused wondering just what to think. Remember that calendars have been altered in different ways in the past 2000 years to a point that it can be difficult to pinpoint the exact year of Jesus' birth. While some theologians say that Jesus' birth could have been as early as 6 BC, others indicate the year 4 AD.

What is most important here is that Jesus' birth, that very first Christmas, is a historic fact. Jesus was born to Mary and to his foster father, Joseph, in a manger in Bethlehem. As for the exact year, we have difficulty with pinpointing the exact year of many contemporaries of Jesus as well, because of either the changing calendars or an imprecise record, or both. Remember, most people in the Holy Land when Jesus was born were illiterate and so had to share the word verbally before finally someone had an opportunity to write down the facts.

In the Apostles' Creed, why does it say, "He descended into hell?"

Many of us learned a host of Christian prayers when we were younger, one which was likely the Apostles' Creed. The Catechism of the Catholic Church outlines quite well what the Apostles' Creed means when it mentions that Christ "descended into hell."

We read in the Catechism that the New Testament affirms that Jesus was raised from the dead, and therefore that Jesus also sojourned in the realm of the dead prior to his Resurrection. Jesus, like all men, experienced death and so joined the others in the realm of the dead, "but he descended there as Savior, proclaiming the good news to the spirits imprisoned there" (CCC 632).

Our faith goes on to teach that the Gospel was even preached to those who died before Jesus walked the earth and instructs you and me that the Gospel message of salvation is brought to complete fulfillment not simply in those who have died after Jesus' Suffering, death, and Resurrection but also in those who lived before Jesus' earthly ministry (CCC 634).

Finally, we recall that Jesus is the Author of Life and has come into the world so that all who hear him will live.

We find great comfort in the fact that Jesus is one of us and that he died and, in doing so, opened up the gates of heaven to all of us, regardless of the era in which we live.

Why was Jesus a descendant of Judah, instead of Joseph or Reuben?

It seems it's currently in vogue to learn about our ancestry in order to ascertain a few things about ourselves. Our ancestry can certainly help provide us an understanding of our own characteristics and mannerisms.

In the case of the genealogy of Jesus Christ (see Mt 1:1–25), we learn that of the twelve sons of Jacob (who also is known as Israel), Judah is one of Jesus' ancestors. Furthermore, we see in v. 6 that King David shares the same ancestor. This is important, because Judah is the son through whom we recognize the kingly succession, an ancient lineage that Jesus Christ brings to fulfillment (see Gen 49:8–12).

Why doesn't the Bible explain Jesus' life between the ages of twelve and thirty?

The Bible is God's revealed word. The Gospel stories underline the fact that Jesus is our salvation. And in these accounts we accompany Jesus throughout his life.

We are familiar with significant moments in Jesus' life, such as his conception in Mary's womb and then being born in Bethlehem. We even have further stories of Jesus being presented in the Temple and then later being found in the Temple at the age of twelve. At this point, we "fast forward" to Jesus' baptism in the Jordan by John the Baptist.

These stories of Jesus are pivotal moments, as described by the four evangelists (who were inspired by the Holy Spirit), that help us understand that the story they are telling is of our salvation in the person of Jesus Christ.

While this explanation may not satisfy your curiosity, trust that Jesus, who is fully God, is also fully human. We know that Jesus did become a teenager and a young adult, just like anyone else who has reached their thirties. Perhaps you and I can find further comfort in the fact that Jesus, who became a man, fully understands the joys and the challenges that you and I are confronted with in daily life. It does not matter whether or not we are five, twelve, twenty, or ninety years old. Jesus understands.

Why is the dove a symbol of the Holy Spirit?

The Bible is very instructive regarding the various symbols of our faith. For one, we are familiar with the descent of the dove upon Jesus at his baptism in the Jordan River. God the Holy Spirit, in the form of a dove, bears witness to Jesus' divinity, as does God the Father in his reply that in Jesus, the Son of God, the Father is well pleased. You may wish to read all four of the Gospels, especially chapter three in Matthew and chapter one in Mark.

While the seven gifts of the Holy Spirit are represented by flames, the dove usually accompanies them. For example, the Sacrament of Confirmation is represented by the dove with seven flames. The dove also symbolizes peace, a peace that is perfectly exemplified in the presence of the Holy Spirit.

How blessed we are that our Catholic faith is full of symbolism which points directly to Jesus Christ and his love for us. Jesus' love for us will never go out of style, nor will the symbols that accompany that love.

Did Mary actually die when she lay down and closed her eyes before her Assumption? I have gotten different answers to this question in the past.

In 1950, Pope Pius XII, the pope at that time, declared the truth that Mary was assumed into heaven, body and soul, when her life was finished here on Earth.

We need to remember here that this truth is not new since 1950, for it is part of the very fabric of the tradition of our faith. Mary had not simply a unique role but the highest role of any Christian; namely, to be Jesus' mother. Mary is the Mother of God! At the Annunciation, that is, when Mary was visited by the Archangel Gabriel on behalf of God (Lk 1:26–38), Our Lady accepted God's invitation to be Jesus' mother. In doing so, we honor, of course, Jesus' conception on March 25, nine months before the great celebration of Christmas. Mary had the highest honor of conceiving Jesus, carrying Jesus in her womb, and then remaining with him as Jesus would share with the whole world that the Gospel is at hand. Humanity finally had hope.

As for the Feast of the Assumption, we acknowledge that Mary did not suffer any of the effects that are associated with death because she participated in Jesus' Resurrection immediately at the end of her life's service here on Earth. How fortunate we are to have such a great mother whom we can imitate.

My religion teacher said that it is mentioned in the Bible that Jesus has cousins. If he had cousins, then why did he give Mary to John to take care of her?

It is true that in the time of Jesus' Passion and Resurrection a family would welcome a widowed relative into the household, especially if she had no other living children. It also would seem that this would be the case with Mary. From the Cross, though, Jesus provides the foundation of our relationship with Mary: Mary becomes our mother.

As Jesus entrusts John to Mary with the words "behold your mother" (see Jn 19:26–27) he also entrusts the Church to Mary. As Mary cooperated in the saving action of God by giving birth to our Savior Jesus, she continues to guide the Church with a mother's care. A mother's care is near, not distant.

Moreover, from the Cross, Jesus indicates the kind of relationship the Church and all believers have with Mary: this is personal. Mary has been made the mother of all disciples—

that includes you and me! Mary's personal relationship with all Christians should give us great comfort that she watches over us daily. The next time you pray the Hail Mary, the Rosary, or another Marian devotion, remember: Mary is right there for you.

The Bible tells of Jesus' brothers and sisters, but Catholics believe that Mary had one child, Jesus. How can this be explained?

It is important that we understand that languages used by people 2,000 years ago did not exactly match the modern languages we use today. For instance, the words used to describe brothers and sisters in ancient Israel extended beyond one's own immediate brothers and sisters to one's cousins. The English language is much more specific in that our words do not embrace such a broad group of people as other ancient terms do.

Moreover, we also understand the truth that Mary, the Mother of God, had only one child; namely, Jesus Christ, Our Lord and Savior. The next children Mary was entrusted with were us, as Jesus spoke to his mother, Mary, and John the Apostle, as he hung on the Cross. Remember how Jesus said, "Woman, behold your son"? Then he said to the disciple, "Behold your mother" (see Jn 19:26). This moment is pivotal in that Jesus entrusts the Catholic Church to Mary, who is our mother.

It is through Jesus' mother, Mary, and his foster father, Joseph, that Jesus would have had extended family, not unlike us. This further underscores the fact that while Jesus is God, he also shares fully in the attributes of humanity, especially having family.

Why wasn't Joseph mentioned for much of the New Testament? Did something happen to him?

We are aware the angel visited Joseph in a dream informing him of the conception of Jesus by Mary, and that Joseph was instructed to take Mary as his wife and to receive Jesus as his foster child. We know, of course, that Joseph was an upright and holy man and that he was a carpenter. However, following Jesus' being found in the Temple over a decade later, we hear of no other accounts of Joseph other than mentions of his relationship to Jesus. While we can't be sure about the rest of Joseph's life, Scripture doesn't note that something happened to him, so we can safely assume that he lived in peace for the rest of his natural life.

The Bible is the revealed Word of God and the Lord gives us all we need to know in order for us to follow him. This being said, so many would love to speculate examples of Joseph's fidelity to God in the Holy Family through particular instances, not to mention, of course, what Jesus' life was like for those nearly twenty years after being found in the Temple, prior to his public ministry. We can pray over each of these questions, recognizing first and foremost God's divine plan for each and every one of us.

Perhaps one of many things you and I can take away from the brief stories of Joseph is his unwavering fidelity to God and to his vocation as foster dad of Jesus and loving husband of Mary. Most certainly Joseph is fittingly the patron saint of all husbands and fathers.

Did the Wise Men think Jesus was one of the many gods (were they polytheists)?

Good question, since there are many understandings of who the Magi were who visited the baby Jesus 2,000 years ago. While there is much speculation, it seems there are a few items that we can understand from our reading of the Bible and our appreciation of ancient history, especially in the area of Persia.

In the time of King Nebuchadnezzar (you may look him up in the Book of Daniel), the Magi were part of his royal court and they interpreted dreams and were specialists in astrology. Here we have the understanding of the Magi following the star, which we get from chapter two of the Gospel according to Matthew. The Magi would have been curious about this star and probably would have searched for its direct location over the Holy Land.

The ancient Persians were polytheists; in other words, they believed in many gods, so we may surmise that so were the Magi.

Having the Magi visit Jesus demonstrates to us that Jesus Christ's arrival into this world was not simply for the chosen people, namely the Jewish people, but for all of humanity. The Magi were ambassadors of a sort for people of other nations that would eventually learn of the Good News of Jesus Christ.

Was the Cross a bad symbol? By that I mean, why did they crucify people on a cross?

As we gaze upon a crucifix, either in our parish church, a chapel, in a classroom, or at home, we are reminded of the depth of God's love for us. Jesus took all of our sins upon himself and died for us so that we may have eternal life.

When Jesus was crucified nearly 2,000 years ago, the motivation of those crucifying him was to punish him. Crucifixion in ancient times was a form of capital punishment, a punishment intended to scandalize others. What Jesus did in his self-sacrifice on the Cross was to change the capital punishment of crucifixion into a symbol of eternal mercy for the human race. Jesus took a symbol which had negative overtones and changed it to a means of our salvation.

Multiple times in the Bible, a race of giants is mentioned. What does the Church teach us about these giants?

In our modern times, we are quite familiar with how human beings come in many shapes and sizes. There can be as much as a four-and-a-half to five-foot difference between two fully grown human beings, and it can happen for a number of reasons.

We also know that faith and science are not mutually exclusive. We are a Church that embraces both faith and reason. This being said, we recognize among various peoples that ethnicity can help determine not only one's skin color but also one's height. This was no different in ancient times. Much had to do with the land in which one lived, as well as a community's diet. Scientific evidence has shown us that various civilizations throughout history had very tall people, while other groups were much shorter. The Bible reflects this reality in various passages that tell us there were people who appeared to be giants compared to others.

When reading these passages, we must be able to disengage ourselves from the "special effects world" of Hollywood and instead immerse ourselves into the "real world" of the human race. Did God create taller people who, at times, could appear to be giants? Just look around you today, and you can see many people who have without question a "height advantage" over the rest of us. These kinds of people are the ones described as "giants" in the Bible.

Why did men have more wives than one back when Jacob in the Old Testament was alive?

The Bible is quite descriptive of the holy men of old who were married to a number of women all at the same time! It's rather unlike our time as Christians, when Jesus tells us that "For this reason a man shall leave his father and mother and be joined to his wife and the two shall become one flesh" (Mt 19:5); that is, marriage is between one man and one woman. Back in ancient times this was not so clear for a number of reasons.

The one reason we should address is that the understanding of marriage was different back then. Communities or families were most concerned about having as many children as possible as quickly as possible for the sake of the family. Also, many children did not make it through childhood because they did not have the advanced health care that we enjoy today. In Jacob's era (Jacob was eventually renamed "Israel"), it was simply the norm for men to have multiple wives.

Thank goodness that over time—and with the specific

instruction of Jesus—we have seen marriage go from a domestic necessity to a sacrament that reflects Jesus the bridegroom married to his bride, the Church.

How does the Church explain God flooding almost everybody in the Noah's Ark story, and then telling Moses to write "Thou shall not kill" in the Bible?

Hopefully we all have had an opportunity to read, reflect, and meditate on the story of the Flood in the Book of Genesis (chapter 7). Much drama occurred prior to, during, and after the Flood—this story has the making of a movie (or two, or three, as we have seen over the years!). The people that Noah lived among had a very violent culture. They were not Godfearing, nor neighbor-loving, except for just a handful of people, namely, members of Noah's family. The story itself illustrates how these people brought the natural consequence of their lack of love and respect for God and others upon themselves: the destruction we read about in the account of the Flood. This may seem like a harsh way to show Noah's ancient culture justice, but God is justified in everything he does.

On the other hand, as we learn from the Decalogue, or the Ten Commandments, we as human beings are not always justified by what we do. Just because something feels good does not mean it is right and just. The very commandment of "you shall not kill" (Ex 20:13) underscores the fact that we communicate our love of God by the way we love and respect our neighbor. God has provided the chosen people with the guidelines by which they keep their covenant with him. Each commandment is not arbitrary, but rather is essential to the integrity of the covenant God strikes with his people. We can even envision the Ten Commandments as a question, with God asking, "You know how much I love you by how I have delivered you from oppression. How much do you love me?" We answer this question by affirming that each human life is sacred.

Why do we go to purgatory and not straight to heaven or hell?

This is a very good question, for many do not understand the meaning of purgatory or others believe that purgatory is strictly a term that was invented by the Catholic Church in the Middle Ages. Purgatory is very real.

As the Catechism of the Catholic Church instructs, purgatory is a state of higher purification after a person's death and before his or her entrance into heaven. When the person dies while in God's friendship, they may be only imperfectly purified. That means that a final cleansing of human imperfection is required before they can enter the joy of heaven. We can refer to Second Maccabees in the Old Testament for some scriptural foundation for purgatory.

Purgatory is distinct from hell or eternal punishment. Before the final judgment there is purification for those who possess lesser faults but are not yet perfectly disposed to enter into heaven and the beatific vision.

This brings me to an extremely important point: In your life, do not simply set purgatory as your goal. That is misplaced confidence for heaven. Jesus provides us with the opportunity to go directly to heaven in his teachings of the

Beatitudes, as well as loving God and neighbor and entrusting the Church with his gifts of the seven sacraments.

How do we know about purgatory if no one has been there and come back? We know this is a period of cleansing, but how do we know this?

We have affirmation of a time of purification and request for mercy and forgiveness of those who have gone before us in in the Old Testament's Second Book of Maccabees. In this story, Judas Maccabeus and his brothers and friends make an offering to God to have mercy on those of their fellow brothers who died in battle but may not have been completely faithful in their service to God. Since the beginning of the Catholic Church, founded by Jesus Christ in his work with the Apostles, we have believed in the truth of purgatory.

We need not have somebody return from purgatory to tell us it exists, but in truth, it does. You see, while God wants us to be with him forever, we also know that we may not be ready to see him face to face when our time here in this world is over. We have the great gift of the Sacrament of Reconciliation, which provides us the ability to be more like Jesus Christ in this world, and for some this is also a sacrament that prepares them to go to God in eternal life.

We have the responsibility to prepare ourselves for going to heaven, but there are times that additional purification is necessary before we can rightly be with God forever. This is called purgatory, which comes from a Latin word meaning "to purify." We do have a connection with and a responsibility to our brothers and sisters who are in purgatory, as our prayers can free them or expedite their presence there. We are also quite aware that our membership in the Catholic Church extends beyond death.

Together let us pray for the souls in purgatory, that through our prayers and the mercy of God they will quickly have opportunity to be with Jesus Christ in heaven forever. This is done through prayer, as well as almsgiving, indulgences, and works of penance in honor of our friends and loved ones who have died. How blessed we are as Catholics to have so many ways in which to participate in the mission of Jesus Christ in showing our world that in Jesus' holy name there always is hope. After all, we are made in God's image and likeness, and he wishes us to be with him forever.

Do priests go to purgatory?

Priests have been chosen by God from among the people of God. In other words, members of the presbyterate are members of the people of God. Therefore, priests (and bishops) who die may also have to undergo the purging process of purgatory, which is necessary before entering eternal life with God (that is, heaven).

God's mercy extends to all of us. While we priests and bishops focus our efforts on getting everyone to heaven, we want to be there with you as well. To be a priest is no guarantee that one has a free ticket to heaven. A priest's responsibility is to get you a ticket to heaven, and thank goodness the tickets are never in short supply! One might say, then how about we all act in such a way that we can just avoid purgatory and go right to heaven? While this attitude is a good start, in the end, we should live our lives not to avoid purgatory but rather to spend eternal life with God.

How long does it take to get out of purgatory?

While purgatory does exist, we also understand it is not simply a place like Steubenville or Atlanta. What we do know is that a purification occurs during the soul's participation in purgatory. Purgatory prepares the soul to be properly disposed to see Jesus Christ and, consequently, to remain with God for all eternity.

This being said, it is, of course, God's decision when one is ready to enter heaven. This may seem like a lot to understand, for you and I live in a world in which we measure time in all we do. In the reality of purgatory what most matters is that one is unworthy to go to heaven but that, through purification, that will not always be the case. We use time in this world to describe purgatory because, as all of us are aware, time is how we understand and measure the sequence of events or ready ourselves for a destination. How blessed we are to know that God prepares us for our final destination, which is heaven.

When Jesus died and the souls went to heaven, what happened to the people who died before? Did they go to heaven?

We know that following Jesus' death and Resurrection he opened the gates of heaven in order that we may enter and spend all eternity with him. As Catholics, we also profess and recognize the truth that Jesus personally went to visit the souls of our brothers and sisters who lived and died before Jesus was born in Bethlehem. Jesus made heaven accessible not just for us who lived following his Resurrection and Ascension to the Father, but also for those who waited for Jesus' arrival in human history. So yes, these souls went to heaven!

Just think how grateful the faithful whose names we read in the Old Testament were when Jesus came for them! We have such great biblical giants like Adam and Eve, Noah, Abraham, Moses, and Elijah who placed their hope in the living God and now they would see him, Jesus the Christ. The story of the faithful who lived before Jesus' birth ends on an eternally happy note. Their hopes have been fulfilled by the same Jesus in whom we place all of our hope.

Why is cremation against our religious beliefs?

Much development has occurred over the decades regarding cremation and its place in the funeral rites of the Church. While our faith teaches us that cremation is not necessarily against our beliefs, it also teaches us that the cremains (what is left of the body after cremation) are sacred and should be treated accordingly.

Following the funeral liturgies and the process of cremation, the cremains must be placed in a sacred location such as a mausoleum or a columbarium, or interred in the ground. Just as we respectfully bury our dead at the cemetery in graves, the cremains deserve the same respect. Placing the cremains on the fireplace mantel, in a locket, or any similar manner, even for sentimental reasons, is not permitted. God has made us body and soul and both should be respected with dignity.

During the prayers at Mass, it says, "He will come again to judge the living and the dead." I thought we were judged once at our death and that judgment was final. Are we judged again?

You rightly point out that together we profess in the Creed that Jesus Christ truly "will return to judge the living and the dead." Regardless of who you and I happen to be, we will sit before the judgment seat of the Lord to answer him about the ways we lived our lives consistent with the Gospel of Jesus Christ, or not. This is not meant to frighten us into blind faith, but to remind us that we are responsible for the lives that Jesus has entrusted us with—both our own lives and those for whom we care. Jesus has given us life as well as the gift of eternal life. We are asked to respond in a grateful and loving manner.

Before I get too off-topic, I'll address the question of being judged more than once. Not to worry, we do not live life in double jeopardy in which we could be judged a second time. God will not second-guess his judgment on you and me. In the end, when Jesus Christ returns to our world for the final judgment, this will bring to conclusion the judgment of the human race and the complete destruction of evil. Not one of us will be overlooked, for each of us is responsible for our conduct.

How fortunate we are that we have a Savior who loves us so dearly and so deeply that he gave his life for us so that there is hope for us at the final judgment. It is quite clear that not one of us can save ourselves. Yet through a little baby born in a manger in Bethlehem to our Mother in Faith, Mary, and her husband, Jesus' foster father, Joseph, we witness firsthand that with God nothing is impossible.

Can people from heaven go to hell?

Heaven is eternal life with God. So the short answer is *no*. To participate in the communion of love between God the Father, God the Son, and God the Holy Spirit should be the ultimate goal for each and every human being. Heaven is the definitive happiness. Heaven has no equal. Once we are with God in heaven, there is no temptation to go anywhere else.

Hell, on the other hand, is "the state of definitive self-exclusion from communion with God" (CCC 1033). Hell is reserved for those who have made a *free choice* not to believe in God or to be converted from sin. In other words, these individuals would not even have made it to heaven in the first place. They chose not to go to heaven.

Through Baptism, we have been united with Jesus Christ and have therefore become children of the light; that is, citizens of heaven. However, we still must live our lives fitting of the gift of the Holy Spirit we have received.

Will people of other faiths be deprived of heaven at the Last Judgment?

We are well aware that God is all-knowing and knows completely why there are so many faiths in the world. We also know that God is perfectly just and merciful.

While what I write next may seem like a "no" answer to your question, it is important for us to understand that we must pray for all of our brothers and sisters throughout the world, especially concerning the promise of eternal life from Jesus Christ. During each Good Friday Passion liturgy's Prayers of the Faithful, we pray for all people regardless of their faith belief. This gives us hope that God will hear our prayers and will exercise the same mercy and compassion to others as he does for us. Jesus Christ came into the world in his Incarnation in order to be the Savior of all humanity.

Our task is to reach out to our brothers and sisters and to share with them the Good News of Jesus Christ and the promise of eternal life offered in the person of Jesus. Together let us pray for our brothers and sisters of other faiths that they may one day dwell with all the saints in heaven.

What is the difference between Catholics, Jews, and Christians, and why did God make it that way?

Understanding the reality of so many diverse religions in this world is a challenging endeavor. Let's keep to the three you listed above. The Jewish people are also known as God's chosen people, because God made his First Covenant with them through Moses. Christians get their name from Jesus Christ himself and have been anointed with the gift of the Holy Spirit at Baptism. The Catholic Church was established by Jesus Christ on the foundation of the Apostles, the first bishops.

As Catholics, we respect other religious traditions, for

each one shares a certain level of truth with the Catholic faith. For instance, in the Prayers of the Faithful at the Celebration of the Lord's Passion (Good Friday), we pray for members of other faiths, even for those people with little or no faith.

We recognize that in Jesus Christ's gift of the Holy Spirit to his Apostles at Pentecost, the Catholic Church enjoys the "fullness of the means of salvation with which he (Jesus) has willed, correct and complete confession of faith, full sacramental life, and ordained ministry in apostolic succession" (CCC 830). In a pluralistic society where some people assert that truth is relative and not certain (remember Pontius Pilate in John 18:37?) we must be ready to stand strong for what we believe.

Why was Peter the one to start the Church?

And Jesus said: "And so I say to you, you are Peter, and upon this rock I will build my church, and the gates of the netherworld shall not prevail against it" (Mt 16:18). How fittingly Jesus established his Church upon rock, for by changing Simon's name to Peter (*Petros*, which is Greek for "stone"), Jesus has established the truth that where Peter is, so too is the Church.

The reason why we recognize that the Church was started with St. Peter is that the true source of the Church, namely Jesus, made it so.

One may ask why Jesus did not hold a Holy Land version of "America's Got Talent" to determine the appropriate leader of the Christian Church, but God's ways are not always our ways of determining strength and leadership. Jesus works through the successors of St. Peter up to our present-day Holy

Father, Pope Francis, as a unifying leader bringing together all peoples. It may not be obvious at first why Jesus chose Peter and not someone else to lead his Church, but we Catholics constantly recognize that Jesus in his divine wisdom established his Church upon the shoulders of St. Peter.

What does it mean when it is said that the pope is infallible?

We live in a world where many people contend there is no truth, only reigning opinion, or that we as human beings have no access to the ultimate wisdom of God. The infallibility of our Holy Father shows you and me that God has a hand in all that we do and remains in constant contact with his Church through the pope, the successor of St. Peter himself.

In his conversations with St. Peter, Jesus gave direct instruction that the Holy Father's responsibilities and authority are not of this world, but of divine origin. Of course, this is not to be taken lightly. For example, papal infallibility does not mean that our Holy Father can declare the suspension of the law of gravity.

Papal infallibility means that the pope, through the gift of the Holy Spirit, can declare doctrine (revealed teachings of Jesus Christ) on matters of faith and morals, such as the Immaculate Conception. This is done with my fellow bishops in union with our Holy Father. In other words, an infallible teaching is a truth to be believed by all our brother and sister Catholics, without qualification.

How long did it take for Christianity to become a worldwide religion as it is today?

The short, simple answer to your question would be: from the beginning of time all the way until now. The more complicated answer is that we are not done. In fact, the Catholic Church is a pilgrim church, which means that as a people, we are journeying toward holiness with our brothers and sisters here on Earth. She is also a missionary church. That is, as long as there are people in the world who have not heard the Good News of Jesus Christ and experienced his mercy and compassion, then our Church has work to do. Over the course of human history, from the Pentecost gift of the Holy Spirit to the Apostles until now, the Catholic Church has evangelized the globe in numerous ways.

To this end, what is most important is for us not to lose our vigor and zeal to share Jesus Christ with everyone, especially those who may happen to be next door.

When did the term Roman Catholic Church first come into being?

Contrary to what many may believe, using the term "Roman" as a description of the Catholic Church is rather recent in our Church's history.

In fact, in the past, "Roman" was attached to the Catholic Church more as an insult than as an objective description. This term was used to improperly identify that the Roman Catholic Church was just another Christian denomination and something lesser than the Catholic Church. For example, things got so contentious and deplorable that in six-teenth-century England there was great division in England over who governed the local Church. At that time, the Church gained many of the great English martyrs, such as St. John Fisher and St. Thomas More.

Did you know that the word "Christian" can be traced back to the first century? We can find it in the Acts of the Apostles, chapter 11, verse 26. But the word "Christian" was not usually used as a description of the Church, only her members. Near the beginning of the second century, St. Ignatius of Antioch provided the first written statement on the Catholic Church as he was preparing to be martyred for the faith.

Over time, the term "Roman" has taken on a more positive connotation, but it does not describe the complete universal church, that is, the Catholic Church. May we all recognize the great breadth of the Catholic Church, both in the East and in the West, North and the South.

Why is the Catholic Bible so different from any other Bible?

It's true that there are many translations of Sacred Scripture, both in English and in almost every language you can imag-ine. We must remember, first of all, that the Catholic Church has had the Bible and all of its books and letters ever since the time God revealed his Word to the various writers who recorded it.

In the beginning, a number of the books and letters were in Hebrew and Greek. Fortunately, St. Jerome, a great transla-tor and doctor of the Church, provided us with the first Bible with all of the books and letters in the same language: Latin. We call this Bible the Vulgate. Following this translation, however, over the course of the centuries, other translations of the Bible were rendered in the common tongue of various cultures and nations. This is where the problem arises.

One of the principal roles of the bishops, who are the successors of the Apostles, is to guard the true translation of Sacred Scripture in all its meaning. This is what we call protecting the Deposit of Faith. In doing so, we bishops entrust others in assisting us in painstakingly translating the Bible into the common tongue of the peoples we serve in our respective countries and dioceses. In other words, the competency of the faithful translation of the Bible falls under the authority of the successors of the Apostles. Jesus, through his very words, provided us with that mandate when he said to St. Peter, "whatever you bind on earth will be bound in heaven, and whatever you loose on earth will be loosed in heaven" (Mt 16:19). Or, more simply, how St. Peter and his successors govern on Earth will also apply to heaven.

We know that there are a number of English Bibles out there that differ partially, if not greatly, from the Catholic translation. Oftentimes, the question may be a translation of a certain word in Greek or Latin into English, but other times it may be that the translators permit the culture in which they live to determine the translation, thus rendering the meaning of the Scripture passages either diluted or meaningless.

When it comes to the English translation of our Bible, we must remember that our society lacks the competency to alter the translation of the Bible, for it is the Bible itself, the Inspired Word of God, which is meant to change society.

How do we know that our faith is true in every way?

Our faith is a gift. We did not invent the Catholic Church, nor did the Creed we profess find its roots in some medieval texts; no, it is Jesus Christ himself who gave us the Christian faith, and it all began with Jesus sharing his Holy Spirit with the Apostles. Jesus Christ, at the beginning of his public ministry, declared that "the kingdom of God is at hand" (see Mt 3:2; Mt 4:17; Mk 1:15). He did not say that one version of the kingdom of God was at hand, but that *the* kingdom of God was at hand. In other words, our Catholic faith is not a human invention, but divinely willed by God.

You may then wonder why we have so many religions in the world. It seems that has been the case for all of human history. But at one point, God intervened in humanity and gave us Abraham and the Jewish faith. Then, finally, he gave us his only Son Jesus Christ and thus began Christianity among the human race.

We are profoundly aware that there are many truths that we share with other religions—such as there being one God—and with Christian denominations—that Jesus Christ is the Son of God. It seems to me that we are easily tempted to insulate ourselves from others when our faith is meant by its very nature to be declared and shared, even if there are some truths in our faith that others do not share with us. At least we can begin with many of our non-Catholic brothers and sisters that there is a God who cares for each and every one of us.

How far back can you trace your succession? Do you know who the original Apostle was in your line?

You and I are taught to "do our homework" in supporting what we wish to share. It is important for us to remember that as we look across different eras sometimes the recordings are not as complete as we would like. I say that because through written confirmation I can trace my apostolic succession all the way back to 472 years ago (the year 1541), to Cardinal Scipione Rebiba.

Now you might ask: what happened to the other fifteen centuries? We need to recall that the sixteenth century was an era of great upheaval and discontent. Think about it. We are speaking of an era in which there was the Protestant Reformation, the Counter-Reformation, military campaigns, as well as sociological challenges like plagues. These trials, among others, handicapped the Church's ability to keep a constant written record. However, despite these challenges, we can trace the apostolic succession of the popes, so we know that my episcopal lineage is intact. As for the specific Apostle, I can safely say it was one of them! Perhaps Peter or James?

Your question touches upon a very significant truth about the Catholic Church, though. There are pillars upon which our faith is built; pillars that, of course, find their firm foundation in Jesus Christ himself. One pillar is Sacred Scripture, also known as the Bible. Another is Tradition, that is, the continuance of the gifts of the Church shared with us by Jesus Christ; gifts that are meant to be protected and defended at all times. And, of course, what you have touched upon today: the Magisterium, or the apostolic leadership in the Church that my brother bishops and I share under the stewardship of the successor of St. Peter, Pope Francis.

How fortunate we are to share with our brothers and sisters the reality that Jesus Christ is the only way, the only truth, and the only life. In no other name can we find our salvation. We are also so privileged that Jesus Christ, Our Lord and God, loves us so dearly that he blesses us with his Mother Mary, our Mother in Faith, who keeps us so dear to her Immaculate Heart. May you and your loved ones find joy and safety in the presence of the Immaculate Heart of Mary.

What is your favorite story in the Bible? Why?

Some biblical images remain in our hearts and minds since childhood, and the Nativity of Jesus remains my favorite story in the Bible. Of course, let us not forget that Jesus was conceived by and born of Mary so that he could offer his life for us, the story which is shared in the Passion and Easter narratives we hear during Holy Week and at Easter.

One of the reasons the Nativity is my favorite story in the Bible is because Jesus' birth is a hope-filled story for such a diverse number of people. Both Mary and Joseph were filled with great joy at Jesus' birth in the manger. The shepherds in the field were amazed at the news that came to them by the angels proclaiming Jesus' birth. Let us not forget the Three Wise Men from the East, who most likely were not Jewish, representing the majority of the human race, which did not believe in the one and only God.

Christmas itself provides hope to our world, reminding each one of us that God cares. During the Christmas vacation, you and I can reach out to others and perform spiritual and corporal works of mercy, for there is no vacation from our Christian life. Together we can encourage others to recognize the truth that in the holy name of Jesus there always is hope.

LITURGY

Why are Catholic churches so big? Why do Catholic priests wear different robes and vestments?

When you and I come together into a church building, we join our brothers and sisters in worshipping God, depending on the size of the church community. For example, some parishes have hundreds and hundreds of families, and so a larger church building is required in order to accommodate the population. Other church communities, such as in small towns, are smaller and require a smaller building.

The origin of the larger church buildings can be traced back nearly seventeen centuries when Christianity was made legal by the Emperor Constantine. The Church leaders of the day adopted the use of the basilicas, which were first used by the civil governments.

As for the color of the priests' and deacons' vestments, the color reflects the liturgical season or the particular feast day that is being celebrated. As the liturgical colors change throughout the year, we are able to identify where we find ourselves in our spiritual journey with the Church. Liturgical colors are our signposts, of sorts.

For example, white is used for Christmas and Easter (as well as on other feast days); red would be for certain days such as celebrating a feast of the Holy Spirit; violet (purple) is the color for Advent and Lent (as well as for All Souls' Day); rose (pink) is worn on Gaudete Sunday in Advent and Laetare Sunday in Lent; and, of course, green is for Ordinary Time.

These colors are a visible reminder that you and I travel together as fellow pilgrims in this world celebrating the treasury of saints and seasons within the Church.

Why do we often hear music in church?

We recognize that at Mass appropriate liturgical music enriches our prayer. In fact, not just any music is permitted at Mass or at worship, because we all know that not all music promotes holiness and our ability to embrace the Beatitudes.

The musical tradition of the Church has ancient roots that even predate the early Church. For example, our Jewish roots remind us that song was integral to the Jewish prayer, especially on the feast days in Jewish communities. The rich treasury of music spans the history of the Church, from ancient chants, to medieval Gregorian chant, to more modern music crafted by some of the contemporary composers of our day.

The music within our Church has great intrinsic value, for it unites us with Jesus in prayer in the midst of our liturgical worship. In a quote attributed to St. Augustine of Hippo, "He who sings prays twice."

Why do the cross and statues get covered before Good Friday and Holy Week?

The covering of the crucifix and statues enjoys a centuries-old history in the Church. The coverings during the Lenten season are a common practice, but not required.

The prevailing mindset of this practice is to help the faithful to focus their attention on the redemptive acts of Jesus on which Lent trains our attention. Just like our Lenten penances, the coverings help us focus on Our Lord's Passion.

The Church is blessed with a treasury of symbols and images, all of which are meant to enable us to grow in faith, hope, and love. The particular season of Lent sharpens our senses to be attentive all the more to Jesus' Suffering and death for our salvation.

Does every church have a relic buried under it? Where does the relic come from and where does it go if the church closes?

Ever since the early days of the Catholic Church the faithful have revered and venerated relics of the saints. This is not to be equated with worshipping the saints but instead we do this to ask their intercession to assist us in living lives faithful to God's Commandments and to request his blessings.

It is fitting to have a relic of a saint beneath the church altar, and this practice has been retained with the most recent General Instruction of the Roman Missal (see paragraph 302). In fact, it is the bishop's responsibility to place the relic under the altar when there is a dedication of the altar or a new church building. At present, we have a new church being built in Carrollton, Ohio—Our Lady of Mercy—and I very much look forward to placing the relic or relics underneath the altar when I dedicate the church.

What would happen to the relics beneath the table of the present altar if they are not to be used? (In your example, when a church closes.) Those relics should be honored in a reliquary, in which the relics are protected and venerated publicly.

Our Christian tradition of venerating relics of the saints is proof positive that the Catholic Church is not limited to her members here on Earth, and that we do not lose our Catholic identity, let alone our heavenly citizenship, when we die. How blessed we are to retain such a profound and holy tradition to honor our brothers and sisters who have gone before us and who still intercede for us in the heavenly kingdom. Next time you have an opportunity to view a relic or perhaps to discover the name of the saint or saints beneath the table of the altar in your church, recall that they are already in heaven praying for us.

A while back, I was able to acquire a relic of Pope St. John Paul II, who was canonized in 2014. I also had the opportunity to concelebrate the Mass with Pope Francis at St. John Paul II's and St. Paul XXIII's canonizations. Relics are a reminder that our citizenship in heaven is timeless.

Why do altar servers carry candles?

Did you know that the carrying of candles at the celebration of the Mass goes back to the earliest days of our Church? The servers who carry candles are part of a tradition that spans over a thousand years, which is much older than the modern English language you and I speak.

The purpose behind carrying a candle goes back even further, for it was not uncommon to have candles at the head of a procession in ancient times in order to "light the way" for a very important entourage or group of people, or a very special person. The candles also inform everyone that something is happening that is very important. Many families light candles for dinner on special occasions, like birthdays or holidays. All the more reason for us to have candles at the celebration of the Holy Eucharist, Jesus' presence with us in his Body and Blood, not to mention in his Word as well.

To be a server carrying a candle is to have a very important role at Mass, for the server is declaring to all that the priest is beginning a celebration that is different from all other celebrations human beings have. At this celebration or gathering, Jesus is making himself present through the priest at the altar and wishes for us to receive him in Holy Communion.

Why is a cross carried down the aisle at the beginning of Mass?

The cross of which you speak is called the "processional cross" or "processional crucifix." Church history instructs that we have had the processional cross at least since the seventh century. A processional cross is a visual reminder that you and I follow Jesus Christ. Just as we may see in processions or parades, groups of people follow banners or flags announcing who comprises the group following the standard.

In our case, at Mass, we are provided catechetical instruction right at the beginning of Mass as well as at the recessional that you and I are here to follow Jesus. In Jesus' presence, you and I find eternal hope, for while it is his will to bring us together in his name, he also wants us to be together again in eternal life in heaven.

Why can't we eat before we go to Mass?

Since the earliest days in the Church, the faithful have practiced the Eucharistic Fast, that is, we prepare ourselves for the reception of the Holy Eucharist. Some 1,500 years ago the fast become a universal practice throughout the Catholic Church. While various modifications have occurred over the centuries, the recent fast guidelines are an hour before Mass for the priest and an hour before Communion for the laity. Separate guidelines are in place for the elderly and sick who may not be able to wait the hour.

Nevertheless, we prepare ourselves during the fast for receiving Jesus' Body and Blood. This waiting time becomes a striking reminder to you and to me that we are going to participate in the saving moment in our lives, Jesus' complete gift of himself to us in the Holy Eucharist.

Think about it: when you play sports you do not exhaust yourself before a game. No, you prepare your mind and body for the coming event so that you will be at your best at the beginning of the game. So too we prepare ourselves in body, mind, and spirit during the fast in order to receive Jesus with our full selves.

Why do Catholics make the Sign of the Cross during Mass?

When we make the Sign of the Cross in church we are providing an outward sign of our profession of faith in God the Father, God the Son, and God the Holy Spirit.

While we make the Sign of the Cross at the beginning and at the end of Mass, many of us also make the Sign of the Cross entering the church building and while exiting. The use of holy water accompanies those sacred gestures. Every time we make the Sign of the Cross we are at prayer honoring the blessed Trinity.

When we begin our day we should first make the Sign of the Cross dedicating the day to the glory of God. Our faith teaches us the Sign of the Cross strengthens us in temptations and difficulties.

Why do we dip our hands in holy water before we enter and leave the church?

There are three reasons, in particular, why we dip our hands in the holy water font and then make the Sign of the Cross with the holy water that is on our fingers. First, it's important to know what holy water is. The fundamental definition of holy water is: "Blessed water, a sacramental whose sprinkling of use is a reminder of Baptism and the means of sanctification" (CCC, glossary). A sacramental is a sacred sign that disposes us to be open to receiving the sacraments, and they render various occasions in life holy (see CCC 1667).

While water has Old Testament roots, as Christians we

sign ourselves first as a reminder of our own baptism.

Another reason we sign ourselves with the holy water is repentance of sin. In other words, asking God for forgiveness as we prepare to enter into our sacred celebration or as we leave the sacred space of the church and go out into the world.

A third reason we sign ourselves is for protection from evil. We ask God to keep us safe, especially, if bad things may come upon us. When we trace the Sign of the Cross with holy water, we identify ourselves as Christians who have great faith that Jesus is with us and will assist us to be more like him.

The use of holy water disposes us and prepares us to receive God's gift of grace and thereby cooperate with it. Holy water blesses people, items, and even events, orienting our lives toward the kingdom of God and our common role as God's ambassadors. How fortunate we are to celebrate our relationship with God who loves us so dearly.

Why are bells rung during parts of the Mass?

Many of our parish churches acknowledge certain moments in the Liturgy of the Eucharist through the ringing of bells. These may include the consecration (epiclesis), elevation, and reception of the Eucharist by the celebrant. Each part of the ritual centers on the Real Presence of Jesus Christ in the Eucharist. The ringing of bells draws our undivided attention to who we have before us at the altar: Jesus Christ.

The ringing of bells at the consecration is considered a liturgical option and is left to the discretion of the pastor. Did you know that this tradition is nearly nine hundred years old? A ringing of a bell informed people the very moment when the act of transubstantiation, or the changing of the bread and wine into the Body and Blood of Christ, occurred. Other times bells have been rung include at the beginning of Mass (the liturgical procession), during the singing of the Gloria, and at the Sanctus (the Holy, Holy).

The Catholic faith is rich in tradition, much of which is evidenced through the various practices we have at the Holy Sacrifice of the Mass. The next time at Mass perhaps it would be helpful to identify the many rituals we have within our Catholic liturgical treasury. Each one of these points to the most important reality: Jesus Christ remains with us always.

Why is the Catholic Church strict on tradition and does not modernize the service like other religions?

Tradition has been handed down to us from the Apostles, and tradition contains our very faith beliefs. For example, we have no right as human beings to change the meaning in the Apostles' Creed, but we have to painstakingly find the right words to articulate the truths it contains. The tradition we practice, of course, is dependent on God's revealed Word in Sacred Scripture and the apostolic succession from the first Apostles—we call that the Magisterium.

As for "modernizing" our tradition, I believe what we need to address constantly as members of the Body of Christ is how we convey that tradition. People can misinterpret tradition as hanging on to the past or appearing to be inflexible when actually we are protecting a truth handed on by Jesus Christ himself. Without tradition, we would not have a Bible. You and I are part of a faith family, which is unique in this world of ours. Still, we should be ever aware of how we may better share that tradition so that more may be involved in our faith. That could be done through improvement of sacred music, or if I may dare say, better attention to homily preparation. I personally am constantly focused on the latter, of course.

Why do we say the same prayers all the time at Mass?

This is a very good question, for it may seem that we as a Church family could be a bit more creative in each Sunday's Mass prayers. Actually, we are. However, there are many constants (permanent prayers or events) at Mass that must remain in place. Why do I say this? Remember, as our faith instructs, prayer is the raising of our mind and heart to God in praise of his glory. But prayer can also be a petition for us to do good, or to thank God for something received, or even to ask God's assistance for others or ourselves. All of this is brought together at the celebration of Mass.

For instance, did you realize that we begin with the same prayer every time Mass begins? We start with the Sign of the Cross. What better prayer is there than to pray to God the Father, God the Son, and God the Holy Spirit? After that prayer, we also ask for God's mercy at the beginning of Mass as we say, "Lord have mercy." On Sundays and feast days, we give glory to God with the Gloria. We can find the roots of that prayer in the Gospel (Lk 2:13). And, of course, we have the readings of the day, which change all the time. Then, we pray our profession of faith, our Creed, in which we recall that the truth is constant and cannot be changed. Next, we share in the Prayers of the Faithful, asking for God's help, knowing that he always listens to us. And then this takes us into the Liturgy of the Eucharist, in which we remember what Jesus did for us and, moreover, how he remains present to us even today just as he was at the Last Supper and during his Passion, death, and Resurrection. We live those moments with Jesus every Mass. We find the richness of this part of the liturgy in Scripture itself. The prayers the priest says change with respect to the liturgical day or season.

During Lent, why does the priest process out in silence on some Sundays, but not others?

The Lenten season is a penitential season. That means that, especially during Lent, we are called to daily repentance. That being said, we recognize how the "Gloria" is not proclaimed at Mass, except on special solemnities during Lent, and the Gospel acclamation is not the usual "Alleluia," but something to the order of, "Praise to you Lord Jesus Christ, king of end-less glory."

The music, also, is subdued for this spiritual pilgrimage of Lent. According to the liturgical books of the Catholic Church, silence has tremendous value in the season of Lent, and it is optional for us simply to proclaim the Communion antiphon at Mass and to process out of the church in silence. This may seem like an oxymoron, but the silence can be deafening within our own hearts, because silence invites us to reflect on the season in which we find ourselves. Lent is not simply limited to the sacred space in which we worship, but extends everywhere outside the sacred doors of the church as well.

For Confirmation, who picked what the gifts of the Holy Spirit were and why did they choose those ones?

God himself chose the gifts of his Holy Spirit we receive in the Sacrament of Confirmation. We receive the seven gifts of the Holy Spirit in order to sustain your moral life and mine as Christians. These permanent dispositions enable us to be receptive to following the promptings of the Holy Spirit.

The seven gifts of the Holy Spirit are: Wisdom, Understanding, Counsel, Fortitude, Knowledge, Piety, and Fear of the Lord. Jesus Christ manifests perfectly the gifts of the Holy Spirit, and these gifts prepare us to receive God's infinite gifts.

Since the pope is also the Bishop of Rome, would that mean that it is his job to confirm everyone in Rome or is there another bishop who would take his place?

You are right in saying that Pope Francis is also the Bishop of Rome. But thank goodness Pope Francis has help with confirmations!

Unlike my situation as the Bishop of Steubenville with fifty-eight parishes under my shepherd's care, our Holy Father, with his office as pope, has been entrusted with over one billion Catholics. At the same time, he is Bishop of Rome. In the Diocese of Rome, there is the vicar of Rome, who is a cardinal, and there are also vicars general. Not unlike in large archdioceses and dioceses in the United States, the chief shepherd of the Diocese of Rome requires additional assistance at various celebrations, including the celebration of the Sacrament of Confirmation.

Still, Pope Francis has the right to confirm in the Diocese of Rome (actually in any diocese in the world for that matter), whenever he is available. I cannot read the pope's mind or anyone else's, but as a bishop I trust he would like to get out to the parishes in the Diocese of Rome more often than already he does. And he already is surprising a lot of people with how many times he has had the opportunity to visit the good people in Rome.

Together let us pray for Pope Francis as he follows in the footsteps of the first pope, St. Peter, a very, very, very good friend of Our Lord Jesus Christ. How blessed we are as a faith community to celebrate the tradition of all of the popes, beginning with St. Peter, and all along having the Holy Spirit speak through Jesus Christ's Church the truth for all to hear.

How old should you be to receive Confirmation?

The age of reception of the Sacrament of Confirmation varies from diocese to diocese. Still, our Church law instructs that Confirmation is to be received at the age of discretion. In other words, about the age of seven is the youngest at which one may be confirmed. The United States Conference of Catholic Bishops, with the approval of the Holy See, decreed that the Sacrament of Confirmation should be conferred on those between the age of discretion and sixteen years of age.

Of course, for pastoral reasons, it is left to the local ordinary (the bishop) to determine the age for reception of the Sacrament. In our case, in the Diocese of Steubenville, I take into consideration the number of parishes, their populations, and their proximity to one another in order to determine the schedule for Confirmation. Our pastors and the members of their pastoral teams are a great help in this decision-making process.

Who do priests confess their sins to?

Priests confess their sins to other priests. Bishops confess their sins to priests, even to other bishops if they wish. The Sacrament of Penance requires a priest to take the place of Jesus in the confessional. While priests are entrusted with the holy gifts of the Church, to be given without reservation to the people of God, the priest also is very much human. Priests share in the fallen nature of humanity and consequently are in need of the same mercy and forgiveness others receive at Confession.

I find great satisfaction in celebrating the Sacrament of Penance as a confessor, but I also experience the healing touch of God on my soul when I participate in the sacrament as a penitent. Please pray for our priests, the distributors of God's saving grace in the confessional, that they too may maintain a healthy practice of frequent participation in the sacrament for themselves.

Can a mortal sin be forgiven?

During Holy Week, we are instructed by the Scripture readings about the extent to which Jesus loves you and me, namely, without end. We all are aware that Jesus suffered, died, and rose from the dead for the remission of sin. Jesus also, in his earthly ministry, gave us the Sacrament of Penance, also known as Confession.

Mortal sin is forgiven in the Sacrament of Penance, but it also is critical that the penitent or sinner confessing the mortal sin should be contrite, or full of sorrow, for such an egregious act. Jesus does not give us the Sacrament of Penance so that he can simply erase sins in order for us to go out and do more of the same. In the Sacrament of Penance, we receive that "spiritual upgrade," enabling us through the grace received in the sacrament to be more like Jesus, thereby avoiding both mortal and venial sin; this way we avoid sin altogether by not giving in to temptation.

The sacred gift of the Sacrament of Penance provides you and me the ability to show others the way of Jesus and to hear his voice. Appropriately so, the Sacrament of Penance should be celebrated by an individual before he or she receives First Communion, thus readying him or her to receive Jesus' Body and Blood in the Holy Eucharist.

How does God forgive all sins in your life, and how can you live like a Christian?

As faithful Christians, we are to journey with the Church in the liturgical seasons by attending Mass and living the theological virtues. The first sacrament you and I receive, the Sacrament of Baptism, has made us God's children, members of Jesus Christ and his Church.

In the Sacrament of Penance, we are forgiven all our sins. Frequent celebration of the sacrament strengthens us to be more like Jesus. "To live like a Christian," as you put it, means that we participate in the daily life of the Church, in word and deed. How better to be a Christian than to receive the gift of Jesus' Body and Blood in the Eucharist? It has been said time and time again: When we receive the Eucharist, we become who we receive.

Who does the Pope confess to?

It would seem that it is impossible to find a suitable confessor for the successor of St. Peter, our Holy Father, Pope Francis. In reality, any priest would suffice for Pope Francis' reception of the Sacrament of Penance and Reconciliation, where the Holy Father is the penitent (the one confessing sin, and requesting forgiveness and God's grace).

While we do not have live feed of Pope Francis going to Confession, we can be confident that he benefits from the same Sacrament of Penance and Reconciliation as we do. It is said that Pope Francis goes to Confession every two weeks.

As the chief shepherd of the Catholic Church, Pope Francis leads by both word and example. This occurs even to the point where our Holy Father reveals that he is a sinner, and like any one of us, is in need of God's mercy and love.

Last year my teacher said that a priest she knew could forget everything after Confession. Does that go for every priest or just him?

I can't speak for the experience of every priest, but I can tell you that the seal of the confessional protects the privacy of the confession. That means that the priest is prohibited from revealing anything that was said in the confessional during the celebration of the Sacrament of Penance. There are no exceptions. The priest himself is Jesus Christ in the confessional and distributes God's forgiveness to the penitent. When the Sacrament of Reconciliation comes to a close, it is done. To put it bluntly: It is finished. The priest moves on to the next penitent.

While it is humbling to realize that we are sinners, how joyful the thought that a priest awaits our presence to share God's forgiveness and grace in our lives. Remember that when you go to Confession you visit a priest, one who has joyfully accepted the role of a good shepherd, which is to guide as many souls as he can to the Good Shepherd. It is important to take inventory of the last time you celebrated the Sacrament of Penance. May you make time to celebrate the great sacrament which is also known as the Sacrament of Forgiveness.

If a person who is divorced goes to Confession and receives God's grace and mercy, why do they still need their marriage annulled to receive Communion?

Recently, Pope Francis wrote about the great need for pastoral outreach by the Catholic Church toward all people, especially those who find themselves in complicated situations with respect to Church teaching. He specifically mentioned those who are divorced and remarried without the benefit of an annulment. Here, let us differentiate between the person divorced, yet not remarried, and the one who is divorced and has remarried without the benefit of an annulment.

It is, hopefully, commonly understood that the person divorced and not remarried is free to receive the Sacrament of the Eucharist as long as the person possesses no impediments preventing him or her from receiving Holy Communion. On the other hand, one who has divorced and remarried without the benefit of an annulment is living in contradiction to Church teaching specifically regarding the Sacrament of Matrimony. Your insight into one going to Confession and receiving God's grace and mercy is a perfect beginning for that individual to have his or her faith life normalized with Church teaching.

Pope Francis recently provided instruction in order that many annulments may be processed more quickly out of pastoral sensitivity for the people petitioning the Church for an annulment. It is my hope that more and more people will take advantage of this new canonical process in order that they may be in full conformity with Church teaching on the sacred nature of matrimony.

It is important to always remember to be open to God's grace and mercy. It behooves us to reach out to all people, especially those who have perhaps had their Christian journey alter course to a different trajectory than the Church would have hoped. Each one of us is made in God's image and likeness and consequently we should extend unreservedly God's compassion and love to all.

If God gives you forgiveness in Confession and it's done again, will you be forgiven again if it was an accident?

Most of us have learned in school or in parish school of religion that Jesus Christ gave us seven "ultimate gifts of grace," or sacraments, of which the Sacrament of Penance and Reconciliation is one. In Confession, we do not just have our souls marked clean of sin, but Jesus fills that vacant space with grace, enabling us to be better people, in other words, to be more like him. This sacrament cannot be replicated by anything we human beings craft or conjure in our words and action. While it is always good each day to reflect on the events of our day and to ask God to forgive us for the times when we have misbehaved through our words and actions, this still cannot replace the Sacrament of Penance and Reconciliation.

You had mentioned, of course, in your question, what if we do the sin again, which I believe many of us know is not terribly uncommon! While I will not get into my own sins or transgressions, please know that yes, even your bishop goes to Confession to a priest.

Frequently, those sins of which we are constantly guilty are a reminder that perhaps we have made these sins a habit in our lives and we should try to address them more thoroughly so that we do not commit the sin again. We should never resign ourselves to the misunderstanding that we cannot stop committing the same sin. That would be, of course, what the Devil wishes for us to do.

You mentioned performing a sin by accident. Actually, for an action to be a sin, it must be deliberate. That does not mean we can never do wrong things by accident, but it's important to consider whether we are putting ourselves in a situation in which something may go wrong.

How blessed we are to have such a great sacrament handed on to us by Jesus Christ and shared through the priests of our Church. Remember the next time you go to Confession you are going to a priest who also is a sinner and needs God's mercy. All the more reason that God's mercy and love will be shared with you in the confessional.

If a person confesses their sins to God by themselves, instead of confessing them to God with a priest, does it still count as the Sacrament of Reconciliation or not?

As Jesus established the Sacrament of the Eucharist, Our Lord also founded the Sacrament of Reconciliation. The Sacrament of Reconciliation occurs only through the priest, who represents Jesus Christ himself. Therefore, the answer to your question is no.

We should pray every day to God, especially at the end of the day. It is also important to share with Jesus that we are sorry for the sins we committed during the day. However, this is not the same as going to the priest for the Sacrament of Reconciliation.

Not to simplify the sacrament, but at the Sacrament of Reconciliation, we have our sins forgiven directly by Jesus Christ through the priest and, in turn, Jesus fills that void created by sin with his grace. That purifying grace is received through the Sacrament of Reconciliation. In the Sacrament of Reconciliation, Jesus not only forgives us our sins, but he repairs the damage we have done. How blessed we are that Jesus always wants to heal us.

Will people who are not baptized still go to heaven?

Baptism is participation in the life of God. In this sacrament we are brought into the Trinitarian life of Father, Son, and Holy Spirit. In Baptism, original sin is destroyed and, as a result, we more fully realize our potential as human beings made in God's image and likeness. Unfortunately, this potential was lost by our first parents, Adam and Eve, with original sin.

We cannot fully reach our potential outside the reception of Baptism. Here you have raised a grave concern: Can one be received into heaven having not been baptized? We are fully aware that we live in a world in which not all people have been baptized. We should pray for them. Of course, we do pray for them throughout the year, especially in the Prayers of the Faithful at the Passion of Our Lord Jesus Christ on Good Friday. This having been said, we also are confident in God's divine mercy. And so, as many among us will die not having been baptized, we entrust them to Jesus Christ's divine mercy.

How fortunate we are to have this holy gift of the Sacrament of Baptism, for Jesus welcomes us into his life. Baptism is not simply becoming a member of a club. No, the Sacrament of Baptism is so much more, for Jesus gives us a gift of the highest blessing of Father, Son, and Holy Spirit, a gift that is with us always. We also know when we sin we fail to remember this beautiful gift. How fortunate we are to have another beautiful gift in the Sacrament of Penance and

Reconciliation, which brings us back to that full embrace of Jesus Christ.

In the meantime, together let us pray for all of our brothers and sisters who have died, baptized and non-baptized, that we may have the opportunity to be together again as one family in Jesus Christ.

Why, during Baptism, do some priests dunk the baby under water while others pour the water over the baby's head?

This is a very good question, for we are blessed with so many profound and beautiful symbols in our Catholic Tradition. Some of these symbols accompany us in the great celebration of the Sacrament of Baptism.

The two forms of this sacrament, as you indicated in your question, are immersion (dunking) and infusion (the pouring of the water on the forehead). The priest or the deacon determine, for pastoral reasons, the proper formula for the individual receiving Baptism. For instance, he may baptize an adult by infusion because the church does not have a baptismal font big enough to baptize them by immersion.

While it is imperative that we use water, especially holy water, what is also necessary is the formula of the words spoken by the baptizing priest or deacon. They must use the words, "I baptize you in the name of the Father, and of the Son, and of the Holy Spirit." These words connect us directly with the words of Jesus that he imparted on his disciples before he returned to his Heavenly Father: "Go therefore and make disciples of all nations, baptizing them in the name of the Father and of the Son and of the Holy Spirit, teaching them to observe everything I have commanded you; and behold, I am with you always, to the close of the age" (Mt 28: 19–20). So, we are sharing Jesus' very words.

There is a tremendous amount of history of the celebration of this sacrament and, of course, it all begins with Jesus being baptized in the Jordan by St. John the Baptist, for Jesus is the source of our baptism.

What happens to babies that die before they are baptized?

As Pope Francis has mentioned frequently, God is an all-merciful God. Baptism conforms us to God in direct participation with God the Father, God the Son, and God the Holy Spirit. It is imperative that a baby be baptized not too long after he or she is born in order to receive this irreplaceable gift. We are aware, though, that some children die before being baptized, and some even die tragically before being born.

We as Catholics believe that God knows each one of us better than we know our own selves. This being said, we also know God wants all of us to be together in heaven. God's love and mercy is too vast and deep for the human imagination to fathom. Therefore, we entrust all of our little brothers and sisters who died before making it to the Sacrament of Baptism to our loving Father who is the very definition of love and mercy. We pray they all are in heaven waiting for us and praying for us.

How many times can you receive the Eucharist in a day?

We recognize that the Eucharist is the central sacrament of the Church, for when we receive the Eucharist, we receive Jesus' Body and Blood. Communion strengthens us and fortifies our resolve to become just like him.

That being said, some may argue: Why can't they receive the Eucharist numerous times each day? Receiving Jesus in the Eucharist once a day is sufficient. To pursue receiving the Eucharist more than once a day may border on the abuse of the sacrament, undermining the eternal and immeasurable gifts we receive at Communion. The gifts resulting from receiving the Eucharist do not dissipate over the course of a day, unlike when you and I eat a meal and then are hungry again hours later.

The answer to your question is that Eucharist should normally be received only once per day, but the Church does provide us with some leeway. There may be extenuating circumstances in which the opportunity to receive Communion arises, such as a funeral Mass or wedding Mass. In this case, you are allowed to receive Communion twice in a day, as long as you participate fully in both liturgies.

Obviously, priests receive the Eucharist more than once in a day, such as on Sunday, but the priest is the exception to this particular rule in that he may be obligated to celebrate multiple Masses on Sunday, as he is both representing Jesus Christ and the people of God at the altar of sacrifice.

I will be taking my First Communion this spring. What's the difference between Communion and Confirmation?

We are profoundly blessed with the seven special gifts Our Lord Jesus gives us, which are the seven sacraments. The Sacrament of the Eucharist and the Sacrament of Confirmation are the last two Sacraments of Initiation. Baptism is the first in this set of important rites.

Eucharist, also known as Communion, is the Body and Blood of Jesus Christ and is the principal Christian liturgical celebration and participation in the Paschal Mystery of Jesus Christ. The Eucharist is the ritual and sacramental action of thanksgiving to God, and at Communion we receive the Eucharist, which is Jesus Christ's Body and Blood.

Confirmation is the sacrament that completes the grace of Baptism by a special outpouring of the gifts of the Holy Spirit. At Confirmation, we are sealed, or "confirmed," in union with Christ and equipped for active participation in the worship and apostolic life of the Church (see CCC 1285).

While the two sacraments are most certainly complementary, it is the Sunday celebration of the Eucharist that is at the heart of the Church's life (CCC 2177).

Congratulations on your preparation for your First Communion this coming spring. How appropriate it is that we celebrate the reception of this Sacrament of First Communion with our younger brothers and sisters in the Easter season, the season of eternal hope and of our participation in the promise of Jesus Christ.

What's the youngest age you can get First Holy Communion?

Did you know that for years it was normal for children not to receive First Holy Communion until they were ten or eleven years old? Don't worry, that idea is not crossing my mind for further discussion, but it is a historical fact. The Catholic Church is quite clear that children who have received the proper instruction, know the difference between right and wrong, and have sufficient knowledge of the mystery of Jesus Christ are able to receive the Body of Christ. Our faith further instructs that we receive Jesus with faith and devotion.

The pastor, the parish catechists, and parents all possess a vital role in properly preparing children for First Holy Communion. As a family in faith, we are obligated to work together so that all children in the parish have received sufficient instruction to be ready to receive Jesus in the Holy Eucharist.

May we together pray for our pastors and their co-workers in the vineyard, including all of the moms and dads, to instruct our young ones preparing for First Holy Communion. This is not an easy time to teach on the mystery of the Holy Eucharist when many in our culture take the narrow view of "seeing is believing."

I remember from my days as a parish pastor how the bonds of a parish are strengthened every time the children come together to receive the Body and Blood of Christ for the very first time. As a bishop, I cherish every moment when I give First Holy Communion, especially at the Easter Vigil.

Why can't everyone have Communion at church?

This is a very good question, for we live in a culture that overly promotes the question: What do we have the *right* to do? Our faith teaches us that we first must be "right" with God. What does this mean? From the earliest times of our Church, the question has been asked who is "right" to receive the Eucharist. We even have records of writings from less than a hundred years after the first disciples of Jesus Christ walked the earth pondering this very question.

One of the great saints of the early Church is St. Justin Martyr. The term "martyr" means that this particular person gave his life for the Church so that you and I may live it today. According to St. Justin, to be worthy of receiving Eucharist, we must have first received Baptism and be living a life in keeping with all of what Jesus Christ has taught. There are requirements our Church has set forth that are consistent with what St. Justin instructed. We also must remember that the person must believe in the Real Presence of Jesus in the mystery of the Eucharist. Jesus' Body and Blood is present in what we seem to see as just bread and wine. As Catholics, this is part of our Creed, and so we have assented to the belief that Jesus is in the Eucharist by saying amen.

I indicated at the beginning that we live in a world where people question whether we have the *right* to do something, but I wish to utilize a different and more relevant definition of "right" in this answer. As your chief shepherd, I encourage us all to exercise our lives not simply by whether we possess a *right* to do something, but more importantly, what is the right thing to do.

Why is marriage between a man and a woman?

Our faith instructs, without qualification, that the Sacrament of Marriage is contracted between a man and a woman for the good of each other and the procreation and upbringing of children (see CCC 1660).

Jesus himself made marriage a sacrament, both through the creation of man and woman, as told in the Book of Genesis, and when he references Genesis in the Gospel according to Matthew 19:5: "For this reason a man shall leave his father and mother and be joined to his wife, and the two shall become one."

Obviously, maintaining this truth in our present culture does not make me popular with everyone, but then I was not elected bishop through a political convention. I was chosen by the Holy Spirit to uphold the teachings of Our Lord Jesus Christ.

There is much more to the argument about marriage being exclusively between a man and a woman from theological, biological, and cultural perspectives, but I would need the rest of this book to explain them!

You may wish to consult our own U.S. Conference of Catholic Bishops' website for additional resources on this topic at usccb.org, in the section titled "Marriage and Family."

At the same time, we should respect those who hold positions contrary to Church teaching, since those people also are made in God's image and likeness and deserve respect as our fellow brothers and sisters.

Regardless of the criticism we may receive, we must always maintain a charitable attitude toward others, as Our Lord Jesus did toward the people with whom he interacted two thousand years ago. We uphold Jesus Christ's teachings, all the while embracing his all-encompassing love.

Why do we need priests?

The priest is present in the person of Jesus Christ as he shares the sacraments of the Church with you. The priest has the role to baptize as well as to confirm (at the Easter Vigil, for which he has received permission from the bishop in his priestly faculties, or at other times with the expressed approval of the bishop). The priest in the Sacrament of Penance, also known as Confession, is present in the confessional in the person of Jesus. No one human being can replace the priest in the confessional as the distributor of God's forgiveness, mercy, and compassionate love—no priest, no forgiveness of sins in the Sacrament of Penance. Of course, without the priest there is no Sacrament of the Eucharist, no Body and Blood of Jesus at the altar. Jesus shared with his Apostles this gift of priesthood and expressed his wish for them not to keep the Gift of the Eucharist to themselves, but to share it with the world. In other words, the priest has put on the mantle of the Good Shepherd and has been commissioned and invited to imitate Jesus to the best of that priest's ability. Most certainly, as Jesus says in the Gospel according to John, "The good shepherd lays down his life for the sheep" (Jn 10:11). Please pray with me for our priests, our spiritual fathers.

How would a student today become a priest?

Well, as I mention to the youth I confirm or during the visits I make to the Catholic schools, you must first keep your mind and heart open to Our Lord Jesus. If you allow yourself to be open to Jesus' invitation, then if you are to be a priest, it will happen. This approach applies to all vocations in the Church. We are blessed with a host of consecrated women and men in our diocese who illustrate Jesus' presence in this world through the evangelical counsels of chastity, poverty, and obedience. Now more than ever in our culture, these gifts resonate in a world that, at times, prides itself in the vain pursuit of individual satisfaction at the cost of virtue. We are also blessed with deacons who assist me in the various parishes proclaiming God's Word and celebrating the Sacrament of Baptism as well as officiating at weddings.

As for the irreplaceable gift of the sacramental priesthood, my dear brothers in this diocese must first consider the priesthood an invitation by Jesus and not some sort of sublime right. We must allow our lives to be like that of St. Thérèse in that we do not allow personal goals or the distractions of the day to get in the way of God's Word. We need to recognize God's presence in all that we do, including prayer. If we do that, we will have a clearer focus on the Christian vocation to which God is calling us. This begins with family. I can see from time to time that family members can actually be the greatest obstructionists to a man considering a vocation in the priesthood. The family must be a healthy nursery in the growth of the Christian vocation for the children, whether it is priesthood, consecrated life, or marriage.

Why are priests not allowed to marry?

This is a common question. For me to respond "that's just how it is" would be an insult to your intelligence. The Catholic priest stands out in our society, and for good reason: he is in the person of Jesus Christ in a very unique way. The short answer is that Jesus is the groom and the Church is his bride. This is the very terminology Jesus used in order for us to understand his exclusive love for us (see Mt 9:14–15). So too are our priests grooms to the Church, as am I, since as a bishop I also am a priest.

Jesus did not marry, nor do we priests marry. This style of life is not so that we are simply more available to the people of God. That is an inaccurate assumption by much of society. The truth goes much deeper than functional availability. For a priest to be exclusively present to the people of God means that the priest lives his life in complete conformity to Jesus' life. The man wishing to be ordained makes promises, promises that shed light on how much he loves Jesus Christ and the people of God. In his promise to be exclusive to Jesus Christ's Church and to no one else, especially regarding marriage, the man professes a public intention to conform himself completely to Jesus himself.

Others argue that allowing priests to marry would provide more priests. To overlook or even dismiss the gift of priestly celibacy in order to increase an imaginary quota loses sight of the reality of what it means to be a priest. A priest lives out his priesthood in exclusive devotion to Jesus Christ and his Church. In doing so, the priest is the celebrant of that great gift of our salvation which Jesus shared with the Church through his Apostles, the Holy Eucharist. We priests certainly are a "band of brothers" in Jesus' name.

Is there any particular reason that priests always wear black when not celebrating a Mass?

We often see priests wearing black, not to mention bishops wear black as well. Truth is, most often we are wearing black under our vestments when we are celebrating Mass. The color of the vestments indicates the time of the liturgical year. However, when the vestments come off, we are back in our black suits or our clerics which, more frequently than not, are black.

You will see me more often than not out in public wearing my black suit even if I am shopping at the grocery store or visiting the hardware store. My clerical suit indicates to others that I am a priest and, who knows, from time to time there are those who may stop me and ask for some spiritual assistance, even to hear their confession.

Of course I own other clothes as well. I do not bike ride in my black suit, nor do I perform yard work in my black suit. Those moments demand outdoor clothes that frequently get muddy and dirty.

The next time you see a priest in his collar, please do not hesitate to stop and say hello to him, for he most certainly would be happy to assist you if you are in need. Also, please pray for our priests, for I am so blessed to have the priests in our diocese, both diocesan and those in religious orders, as my brothers. Our primary job is to enable you to become a saint and to get you to heaven.

How does the bishop know so much about God and the Church?

On September 10, 2012, through the Sacrament of Ordination, I received the three functions and powers to teach, to sanctify, and to govern. However, that holy moment of receiving God's grace did not provide me with an IQ of 250. As a matter of fact, I have learned through the years of my episcopal ministry in a profound way my limitations as a human being striving for holiness.

You and I need Jesus Christ. Every day we need him. Every day I celebrate Mass and pray the Office of Readings, which is the common prayer of the Church and which I have promised to pray daily. I also take a Holy Hour with the Lord and have opportunity throughout the day, albeit sometimes briefly, to reflect and meditate on parts of the Bible. Still, with all of this prayer time, I also realize the temptation for the bishop "to live in a bubble." Our Holy Father, Pope Francis, is quite clear that my brother bishops and I must get out into the world and be with our people. The odometer on my car certainly illustrates the fact that I do not stay in one place too long!

My brother bishops are a great source of wisdom for me as I exercise my ministry, as are my brother priests as we share our priestly ministry as celebrants of the Holy Eucharist, and as they serve as pastors of their respective parishes. I also receive insight and support from the outstanding people on my chancery staff in Steubenville. I also have the opportunity to visit with parish communities and their families, as well as, of course, our schools. Further assistance to my ministry is my getting out, even on the street in Steubenville, Marietta, or Ironton, to see the people. Yes, I even learn a lot when attending a high school football game.

Having said all this, my conclusion to this is simple: my beginning to know so much about God and his Church is my self-knowledge that I really don't know as much as I should. This attitude is humbling, but also essential to a shepherd in our Church who embraces the true faith that Jesus Christ is the Son of God who suffered, died, was buried, and rose from the dead in order that you and I may have eternal life. Jesus will never leave us and wants us to understand more fully the depth of his love.

Have there always been bishops in the Church?

The short answer is yes. We know from the Bible that Jesus ordained the first bishops, who also were known as the Apostles. Through the gift of the Holy Spirit, other bishops followed (or succeeded) these Apostles as the "first bishops" shared the episcopal ministry with the bishops who followed them.

In other words, there is an unbroken chain or tradition between myself and my brother bishops and the Apostles who walked with Jesus nearly two thousand years ago. This is edifying, for the Eucharist, which we celebrate at Mass, depends on the ministry of bishops. As the priest is an extension of the ministry of the bishop, it is through him that we have Jesus'

Body and Blood in the Eucharist at the altar.

How blessed we are to have within Jesus Christ's Church, the Catholic Church, the great gift of the Magisterium, which is made up of Pope Francis, who is the successor of St. Peter, and his brother bishops.

What is your favorite part of the Mass and why?

It seems to me that most people have a favorite part of the Mass, whether we are speaking about the music, the homily (yes that can be a favorite part of the Mass), or the readings. In fact, my favorite part of the Mass is the Liturgy of the Eucharist and, in particular, the Eucharistic Prayer. I say this because the Body and Blood of Christ, the Eucharist, unites us with Jesus Christ. In this spiritual food we become who we receive. The growth we experience as Christians completely depends on our reception of the Eucharist, especially the frequency with which we receive Communion.

May we not forget that Jesus himself instituted the Eucharist at the Last Supper. Do we not hear at Mass each and every time, "Do this in memory of me"? Jesus has given himself in the Sacrament of the Eucharist, and we should be forever thankful for this gift, which exceeds all expectations. I am profoundly grateful as a priest and bishop to be God's instrument at the moment of the transubstantiation when the bread and wine become Jesus' Body and Blood at the altar. This sacred moment is for your salvation and mine.

How did you become a bishop?

The short answer is that God called me to be a bishop. The longer answer involves the process in which the Catholic Church carefully listens to the Holy Spirit in the choice for our bishops. This occurs in a number of ways, from prayerful choices to inquiry with other bishops and individuals familiar with potential candidates. It is a very involved, and at times painstaking, process. You see, the Holy Father determines through the gift of the Holy Spirit who the men are who are to follow in the footsteps of Jesus, as successors of the same Apostles Jesus called nearly twenty centuries ago.

For a U.S. bishop, extensive work goes into the process here in the United States as well as in the Vatican at the Congregation of Bishops, who are a group of bishops who assist Pope Francis in his governance of the church as the Vicar of Christ.

Needless to say, I was very surprised to receive the phone call from the apostolic nuncio (sort of like the Holy Father's ambassador to the United States) on June 26, 2012, informing me the Holy Father wanted me to be your bishop. What went through my mind is similar to your question: "How did I just become a bishop?" After that, I did some research to better understand where the Holy Spirit was sending me: the Diocese of Steubenville.

Do scapulars actually keep you from hell?

From what I have read, scapulars began with the Benedictine Order and were eventually adopted by other religious communities. Today, we have men and women who are not members of professed or consecrated communities wearing scapulars as well.

The scapular is a symbol of "putting on Jesus Christ." Another way of putting it is that we wear the "yoke" of Christ. We are reminded to become more like Jesus in our everyday lives and to keep him ever close to us.

While your question focused on the avoidance of hell, what would be more fitting is to say that scapulars point us toward heaven. Scapulars direct us toward the good things that Jesus has given us.

For those who like to know the origins of words, the word "scapular" comes from the Latin "scapularium" or shoulder cloak. How blessed we are with the opportunity to physically put on a small garment reminding us that you and I have in our baptism put on Christ.

LIFE IN CHRIST

What do I have to do to be a good Catholic?

It seems to me this is a question common among Catholics as we explore our very identity as Catholic Christians. I say this because being Catholic does set us apart from other Christians in important ways, the celebration of the seven sacraments for one. Still, the approach we take here is not one of elitism, but of our relationship with Jesus Christ himself. Jesus wants to be part of our lives.

The easy answer to your question may seem to be to follow the Ten Commandments and be nice to people. It's a good start, but our faith goes much deeper than following rules; it's about our very relationship with God. That is why we attend Mass every weekend, for it is there that we receive Holy Communion, Jesus' Body and Blood, and we hear God's very words in the readings. Your going to church is your way of saying: "Jesus, thank you for loving me. I love you, too." Also, by following our Church's teachings, we show Jesus that we trust him and are grateful for his founding our Church, as we journey with Jesus into this third millennium of Christianity.

The teachings of Pope Francis are the same as St. Peter teaching us himself.

We also should pray every day and, of course, imitate Jesus by being kind to people, especially members of our family. While the Ten Commandments were given to Moses by God, we also have the Beatitudes, which came from Jesus himself. These instruct us in what we should do to be more like Jesus, as we set an example for others. As Jesus says, we should first love God and neighbor as ourselves (Mt 23:39).

How do you keep your relationship with God healthy?

You and I are constantly discovering new ways to deepen our relationship with God as members of his children. We keep our relationship healthy first of all by being faithful to God and his Church. For instance, a healthy prayer life strengthens a healthy relationship with God. Frequent attendance of the Holy Sacrifice of Mass strengthens our Christian identity as we hear the Word of God and receive the Body and Blood of Jesus Christ, thus becoming who we receive. In our Mass attendance we also strengthen the faith of our brothers and sisters as they see us present at the sacred liturgy.

Daily prayer is critical in our healthy relationship, for we deepen our faith in our daily conversation with God. We can do this through the prayers we learned as children, such as the Lord's Prayer, the Hail Mary, and the Glory Be, as well as the devotions such as the Rosary and the Divine Mercy Chaplet and prayers for the intercession of the saints, such as the prayer to St. Michael. Moreover, it is important that we do not always pray these prayers alone but with family, thereby strengthening one another in the Catholic faith.

Frequent participation in the Sacrament of Penance is critical, as Our Lord Jesus is waiting in the confessional to forgive each one of us for our sins and to strengthen us in his grace. Each time we visit the Sacrament of Penance we are further strengthened in our Christian calling to be more like Jesus.

Since we do not go to the Sacrament of Penance every day, it is important that we perform an examination of conscience each evening before we go to sleep, reciting, perhaps, the Act of Contrition, in which we express our sorrow for the mistakes we made that day and then perhaps following the prayer with one of gratitude for the gift of life and the people God has placed so generously in our lives.

The common denominator here? To keep our relationship with God is to encounter Jesus daily.

How do we know God's will for us?

Jesus Christ provides us the perfect attitude with which to determine God's will: humility and obedience. Jesus gave us the Lord's Prayer, underscoring the fact that you and I have a role in doing the Father's will. Jesus gave us the instruction in the Beatitudes: "Blessed are the pure of heart, for they shall see God" (Mt 5:8). In other words, the right attitude removes distractions and gives us laser focus on God's will for us. Still, this entails much effort, for the distractions in this world are plenty and can be quite convincing if we do not exercise clarity of faith, critical thought, and prudential judgment.

Prayer provides us the ability to discern God's will for us, for prayer is conversation with God. While both personal and communal prayer is integral to our spiritual journey, the sacraments are critical to our discernment process. For instance, reception of the Holy Spirit at the Sacrament of Confirmation equips us for active participation in the Church. Frequent reception of the Body and Blood of Christ strengthens our resolve to do God's work, and we should not forget that the Sunday celebration of the Eucharist is at the heart of the Church's life. Frequent celebration of the Sacrament of Penance inclines one's heart to the will of God, creating space for Jesus.

For one who is considering a priestly or religious vocation in the Church, you may want to speak with a priest or a religious sister or brother. They would have traveled a similar discernment path as you and should be able to assist you in asking the right questions.

To put it simply, in order to know God's will for you, you should make room for Jesus in your daily life. Jesus is always with us. Jesus continues to knock on the door of your heart and mine. We find comfort that the Catholic Church has a treasury of ways, gifts from God himself, in which we can correctly respond to his invitation.

What is the best way to incorporate God in my life when I do not have any free time?

It seems for each one of us that there is not enough time in the day for all of the plans and projects we have. We must prioritize. So, too, we must place God at the forefront of our daily priorities as well, for he is the One who has given us life and loves us more deeply than you and I can imagine. In planning our daily routine, we should begin the day thanking God for our life, for our family, and for the day itself. We thus begin the day in a spirit of gratitude.

Asking the Lord to bless the food we are to receive also reminds us of God's generous nature in providing us with the food we eat. That spirit of gratitude should continue throughout the day and should also be incorporated in our prayers before we go to sleep at night, thanking God for the day as well as asking for his forgiveness for those moments in which we were less than charitable to our fellow people.

The celebration of Mass occurs each day in our parishes, so for those who have the availability of transportation, I encourage them to attend daily Mass or at least a number of times during the week, in addition to their Sunday attendance. We can also pray various Catholic devotions, such as the Rosary. Some devotional prayers only take a minute or two and provide us with the knowledge that we are not alone and that the saints in heaven are praying for us as well. This all comes down to priorities and planning our day in a way that allows us to recognize God's presence in our lives. Remember, God always has time for us.

Is it hard to try to listen to God's will and understand how to carry it out to other people?

There are times it is very easy to listen to God's will and to share it with others. Other times it can be quite difficult. We know from the first chapter of the Book of Genesis that God created this world to be good. And yet, we have a way of going against God from time to time. God has given us free will. While he does not force us to follow him, through the gift of Jesus Christ, we are shown the way.

Many cultures may accommodate or oppose the sharing of the Good News of Jesus Christ (evangelization). We recognize even in our own society Catholics who find it difficult to publicly live or promote their faith. Pray for them. While we cannot read their hearts, we can assist them spiritually to get beyond the impediments in their lives that prevent proclaiming the truth of Jesus Christ.

Carrying out our faith is a lifelong endeavor. You and I should be grateful that Jesus has entrusted us with the truth that he is the only way, the only truth, and the only life.

How should we help children in need?

I congratulate you for asking such a profound question, for the very nature of the question tells me you want to reach out to others your age. Of course, while you do not hold a steady job right now (other than being a student) your options are limited, but not necessarily ineffective.

I would suggest that you first look around you and identify those children in need. It is good for us, at times, to begin with those with whom we may be familiar.

You also may wish to contribute to or begin an outreach to other children. I recall, as a pastor, when the youth in my parish indicated that they wanted to attend World Youth Day in Australia, we attempted to find ways in which to raise money for such a project. The students arranged with recycling companies to buy back used paper and ink cartridges that they collected. You would be amazed how much money they were able to raise for a successful trip to World Youth Day in Australia, all because they exercised ingenuity and creativity.

Finally, and most importantly, please pray for the children—not just in the Ohio Valley but throughout the world—who are living in very difficult situations. Our prayers do help others, even if we are not there to witness the end results. In the Lord's Prayer we say, "Thy Kingdom come, thy will be done," which means you and I have a role in bringing heaven to others.

How can I become a saint?

Each one of us wishes to be together in heaven someday, and we demonstrate that desire through our own words and actions here. The Catholic Church acknowledges a saint indicating the heroic virtue they have lived and their fidelity to God's will. One's personal holiness sets an example for others, as a person of hope, especially in those times which may be most difficult to be a Christian.

I encourage you, in addition to your Mass attendance and daily prayer, to read the lives of the saints. You may wish to begin with a particular saint whose attributes or character may be similar to your own. The Catholic Church has such a beautiful treasury of saints, and the accounts of their lives is impossible to exhaust in our reading.

You'll be surprised by how so many of the saints who have gone before us are just like you. Each and every one of them demonstrates to us how we may say "yes" to God with our own lives. Beginning our day with prayer, asking God to make us holy, and being kind to others is a perfect start to becoming a saint.

If God was with us all the time, why do we feel sad or get hurt when we think we are on the road to heaven?

You are right in saying that God is with us all the time. Unfortunately for ourselves, we don't always pay attention to God being with us all the time. This is a reminder of our incompleteness without God's presence. In other words, as a result of original sin, when Adam and Eve, our first parents, decided they did not need God, the world was sent into disarray.

What I mean by disarray is that paradise was taken away from us. The results of the sin of our first parents resonate throughout the world in the form of our being sad or hurt or even recognizing the bad things that happen in the world to this day. We know as Christians, though, that this is not the end of the story. In Holy Week, we remember Jesus' Suffering, death, and Resurrection in order that paradise be returned to us. It is Jesus whose enduring presence accompanies us in our sadness and provides healing when you and I hurt. In other words, Jesus completes us. So, may we remember the next time that we are hurt or sad that God is with us and find great comfort that he knows how we feel. He is always listening.

How do I help somebody I know who is going to become a Christian?

First of all, the best way you and I can assist another person to become a Christian is first to live our own Christian lives. This may be a good time for you to discuss Christianity with that person, which also means you may need to do your own homework by reading the Youth Catechism of the Catholic Church (YOUCAT). Personally, I would begin with a prayer from the Bible, the Lord's Prayer (Mt 6:9–13). This was the prayer given to us by Jesus Christ himself.

You may wish to visit with the individual and discover any questions he or she may have about the Catholic faith. It is not wrong for you to reply "I don't know" to a question when you do not have the answer readily at hand. I, too, from time to time, perform some level of research in my writings or even in answering questions posed to me. I owe it to the other person to share the truth of Jesus Christ, Our Lord and Savior, the Son of God.

Remember, because of our baptismal gift, you and I are ambassadors for Jesus. You need not be a member of the clergy or the consecrated life in order to share the Gospel.

How do you balance reaching out to others who have no faith and making holy, faith-filled friends?

There is an old saying that "no man is an island." I am blessed with many friends, some who are not Catholic and others who are not even Christians. Most of my friends are Catholic, and no one questions my firmness in the faith we profess at Mass.

Still, we live a faith that is meant to be personal and communal. All of us have been made in God's image and likeness, so each person should be treated with the dignity of a child of God. We do not disown or compromise our faith in order to be liked by others, but we cannot afford to insulate ourselves from a world in dire need to hear the Gospel of Jesus Christ and the Easter hope of our eternal salvation.

That is where evangelization comes into our lives. When Jesus told Peter and the disciples to "put out into the deep," he was not telling them to stay in their comfort zone and bother no one, nor make new friends. If, as my motto (faith comes from hearing) from St. Paul's Letter to the Romans is to resonate through our words and actions, then we need to make new friends and acquaintances who deserve to hear the truth of the God who loves them so dearly.

How does one figure out God's plan for their life?

How many of us following graduation, whether high school or even college, sense a great uncertainty in our lives? This is a reminder that you and I are not sovereign or, in other words, we do not have complete control over our lives; we must, in the end, depend on God.

One thing we should always remember is to keep the lines of communication open with God. This occurs in numerous ways: by attending Mass at least every Sunday (or Saturday evening), or even daily; taking time out for daily prayer; having a good heart-to-heart with our parents (yes, parents are outstanding resources for our future!); and of course knowing our own abilities.

While we all want to envision our future, we must realize that discernment and uncertainty are part of the process. It has been said that discernment is the choosing between two goods. Many of you who graduated from high school realize that there are many options in your life, which, of course, does not make it any easier for you to plan your future. Just remember that God has a plan for you and wishes for you to listen to him in order to see where he wishes you to go.

When I graduated from high school, I was uncertain whether or not the Lord was asking me to become a husband and dad or a priest. Did Our Lord Jesus surprise me in making me a bishop three decades later! This was most certainly not on my personal radar, but I am so grateful to God to be your bishop in the Diocese of Steubenville. To all of you trying to determine where your life is taking you: trust that I will say a special prayer for you and ask that you keep me in yours as I try to be the best shepherd possible for you.

Why are saints important to us?

We know from the Book of Genesis that God created us in his image and likeness: "God created man in his own image, in the image of God he created him; male and female he created them" (1:27). You see, we were made in God's image and likeness and shared friendship with God until original sin was introduced into the world by our first parents, Adam and Eve. However, in his compassionate love, God sent his only Son, Jesus Christ, to destroy original sin and to recreate us in God's image and likeness, as we are in the Sacrament of Baptism.

That being said, we recognize in the saints that men and

women are holy when they are in union with God. The saints enjoy eternal life in heaven. In other words, God has given you and me the capacity to be saints. God has gifted the Church with a rich tradition of saints right from the time when Jesus walked with his friends in the Holy Land.

Our faith teaches us that we are capable of imitating those saints who embraced the holy life to be like Jesus. In a way, saints are our "spiritual GPS," guiding us through our own individual pilgrimage here on Earth. Many of us have our favorite saints, those we aspire to imitate or perhaps we share similar likes and characteristics. One may choose for a confirmation name a saint who he or she wishes to imitate or perhaps admires for their personal witness to Jesus.

The lives of the saints give us a peek at the vocational calling you and I have to be saintly. The lives of the saints extend throughout all Christian vocations and teach us that no matter our worldly vocation in the world, we most certainly are called to a saintly life. The saints give us that flesh, bone, and soul example of how we may embrace that sacred calling.

How does the pope decide who will be the next saint?

The canonization process (the procedure for the declaration of a saint) is one many people may not understand. The pope's role in the entire endeavor is absolutely necessary.

The Holy Father approves the official research into a person's life and virtue five years following that person's death. The ordinary, or bishop of the diocese, of the individual investigates the deceased individual providing the petition to the

Holy Father to begin the cause for beatification and canonization. The pope investigates the cause through various offices, mainly congregations and dicastories of the Holy See.

There are four stages in which the process continues: First of all, if the process of the person is approved to go forward, that individual is declared a servant of God. Next, if certain heroic virtues have been recognized by the Holy Father, this person will then be called venerable. Third, if there is a proposed miracle that has been validated by the Holy See, the person is considered blessed (has been beatified). Finally, following the beatification, if a second miracle is discovered, the miracle again is examined through theological and scientific commissions. If the warranty of the second miracle is approved, the Holy Father declares that person a saint (the person has been canonized).

You see, great effort goes into the process of beatification and canonization, which is exclusively the domain of the pope himself.

Why were faith, hope, and charity chosen as the theological virtues?

"For now we see in a mirror dimly, but then face to face. Now I know in part; then I shall understand fully, even as I have been fully understood. So faith, hope, love abide, these three; but the greatest of these is love" (1 Cor 13:12–13). These words from St. Paul's First Letter to the Corinthians underscore the fact that these virtues of faith, hope, and charity relate directly to God, and are thus called "theological."

As the Catechism of the Catholic Church instructs us:

the theological virtues "dispose Christians to live in a relationship with the Holy Trinity. They have the one and Triune God for their origin, motive, and object. The theological virtues [of faith, hope, and love] are the foundation of Christian moral activity; they animate our actions and give them special character" (1812–1813).

These gifts from God enable us to act as God's children. In our call to holiness, the theological virtues enable us to imitate the Father, Son, and Holy Spirit. As we are taught by the Church, Jesus Christ's own self-revelation and self-giving is the foundation of the theological virtues.

Why do we have the corporal and spiritual works of mercy?

Let us list the spiritual works of mercy and the corporal works of mercy:

Corporal Works of Mercy
- feed the hungry,
- give drink to the thirsty,
- shelter the homeless,
- visit the sick,
- visit the prisoners,
- bury the dead,
- give alms to the poor.

Spiritual Works of Mercy
- instruct the ignorant,
- counsel the doubtful,

- admonish sinners,
- bear wrongs patiently,
- forgive offenses willingly,
- comfort the afflicted,
- pray for the living and the dead.

By performing any of these works, we live our daily lives imitating Jesus' earthly ministry. For instance, Jesus was constantly reaching out toward others through forgiveness, comfort, and prayer. In the same way, we can reach out to others and enable them to be more like Jesus. In performing these works of mercy, we answer the call of Jesus in the Gospel passage, "for I was hungry and you gave me food, I was thirsty and you gave me drink, I was a stranger and you welcomed me, I was naked and you clothed me, I was sick and you visited me, I was in prison and you came to me" (Mt 25:35–36).

Performing these works of mercy is our answer to Jesus' invitation to care for others. By performing these works of mercy, you and I become the hands of Jesus reaching out to friends and neighbors, informing them that they matter in God's eyes as well as ours. Remember, these works of mercy have their foundation in Jesus Christ himself.

Why do we fast?

Did you know that fasting can be traced back in our history to well before the chosen people (our Jewish roots as Catholics) left Egypt and traveled to the Holy Land? Fasting is not a concept that is purely Catholic, but we practice it as a method of self-discipline and interior penance.

Many of us are familiar with the two principle fasting days of Ash Wednesday and Good Friday. Fasting is a reminder of how Jesus fasted for forty days and forty nights before he began his public ministry of teaching that the kingdom of God is at hand, as well as performing miracles and healing people's illnesses.

We fast, too, as a form of penance or a sign of sacrifice for forgiveness, or to remind ourselves how much you and I need God. No human being is sovereign; we all need Jesus.

Perhaps the next time we fast, we should try not to focus so much on being hungry. When we fast on certain days, may we draw more on how much we need Jesus.

Why do we have to go to church every Sunday?

This is a very good question, for many people wonder why they have to go every Sunday when so many Catholics and non-Catholics have decided not to. Attending Mass every Sunday (or Saturday evening) is actually one of the Five Precepts of the Church. What is a precept? A precept is a general rule or command. For our purposes here, the precept enables us to grow in the love of God and neighbor. Your question is regarding the First Precept of the Church, which is, "You shall attend Mass on Sundays and Holy Days of Obligation and rest from servile labor." What we do when we attend Mass every Sunday is sanctify that holy day with our own lives as we continue to grow as Christians. Here is a good question: What in our lives could be more important than receiving the Body and Blood of Christ each week?

Recall how, for many of us who participated in team sports

or band, we had to practice before the next game or concert. Well, by going to Mass every week, we become better Christians and most certainly have a better understanding of Jesus' "game plan" for each and every one of us, as well as for the human family. As in sports, if you continue to miss practice, you become less and less an effective member of the team. While Mass is much more than practice, I hope you get the point.

Just for your information, the other precepts are: You shall celebrate the Sacrament of Penance at least once a year; you should receive the Eucharist at least once per year during the Easter season; you shall observe the days of fasting and abstinence (especially during Lent) established by the Church; and the final precept, you shall help to provide for the needs of the Church; that is, assist your pastor in the parish community to be faithful Christian stewards among the community.

Why is the Catholic faith so strict about Lent?

Our faith teaches us that the season of Lent is meant to be the primary penitential season, during which we imitate Our Lord Jesus who spent forty days in the desert in fasting and prayer. We do the same with our Lenten sacrificial practices.

For one, we fast and abstain from eating meat on Ash Wednesday and Good Friday. The remaining Fridays in Lent we abstain from meat. During Lent we also embrace penitential practices—sacrifices that are a reminder of how much we need Jesus. Whether or not you give up Doritos for Lent (now you know one of my childhood penances), or pick a time each week in which you assist our brothers and sisters in need (this would be a more adult practice, unless perhaps it is done as a family), these moments of sacrifice provide us a greater awareness of how much Jesus sacrificed for you and me to have eternal life.

Our Catholic faith also reminds us that the Lenten season is a "climb up the Easter Mountain." This phrase serves to remind us that to attain any worthwhile goal requires great sacrifice. Lent is meant to be a pilgrimage with Jesus and the rules and expectations in this season are meant to give our attention to Our Lord Jesus who loves us more than you can imagine.

Does everyone have their own guardian angel or do people share guardian angels?

The Catechism of the Catholic Church defines a guardian angel as an angel "assigned to protect and intercede for each person" (glossary). It seems to me the answer is in the One who assigns the angel and for what purpose the angel is assigned. God loves us more than we can know; he also has at his disposal heavenly beings who we cannot see or recognize with human eyes and ears. We should take great comfort that Jesus loves us so dearly that he will go through extraordinary means to guide us and to keep us safe. The Old Testament is full of stories of helping, or guardian, angels. Even after the Church was established by Jesus Christ, the earliest Christians recognized the ongoing presence of guardian angels.

The Church does not teach that guardian angels are shared—indeed, the fact that you have your own guardian angel is part of what makes it so special! Also, we believe that the guardian angel, by its very name, serves us as a guide and a guardian. That being said, we do not know whether or not each of us has only one or more than one guardian angel. As your bishop, I just ask you do not intentionally test their abilities, just be grateful for their presence. Guardian angels are a sure sign that we are never alone.

Why did God command the Jewish people to not eat certain "unclean foods," but we are allowed by the Catholic Church to eat them today?

This is a very good question, for to this day there are people of different religions who have dietary restrictions with respect to their particular faith. We, as Catholics, are no different. But first, you refer to the instructions provided to Moses and Aaron in the Book of Leviticus, chapter 11.

The dietary restrictions given to the Jewish people were external symbols of their fidelity to God's covenant with them. God would remain faithful to the covenant, and he expected the people to hold to their end of the agreement as well. While some may explain that some forbidden foods actually could be dangerous to the people in ancient times, the deeper spiritual meaning was that the people would remain faithful to God's covenant.

Jesus Christ, the Son of God, has fulfilled the Old Covenant that was made through Moses, and so there are no longer restrictions, such as food deemed unclean, for religious purposes. However, in acknowledging how Jesus sacrificed all so that we may have eternal life, we have our own Lenten penances of fasting and abstinence. These outward penances are meant to make an interior impression of how much you and I love God and continue to acknowledge all that he does for us.

Why did the Prodigal Son's father welcome the foolish son with such warm and kind feelings, not throwing a party for the son who stayed and did work for his father?

It appears the son who stayed at home had the same question as you. The father's answer to that son indicated the father's great love for both sons. In no way does the father support the wayward actions of the other son. The father does not explain away or find a flimsy excuse for the prodigal son's actions, but uses the situation to show that his heart remains completely open to the both of them.

Here Jesus communicates to all of us the Father's love God has for us. His love is full of mercy and compassion, even when we find ourselves in the most unfortunate of circumstances.

The parable of the Prodigal Son is considered by many the greatest story ever told. I would like to go further in saying that it is a story about the greatest love there is—the love God has for us.

However, Jesus did not tell this story to his friends to entertain them. No, Jesus shows us the depth of his love for us and that we are commissioned to do the very same as fellow Christians. Our Christian lives are not static, but active and full of life. In forgiving others, especially family, we share the very love and compassion of the father in the parable.

Are Catholics who live in the United States presently being persecuted for their faith? If so, how?

This is a particularly timely question. As a bishop—as a leader in the Catholic Church—I have the ability to view the "larger picture" of the Church in our beloved country. Persecution comes in many forms and at times can even attempt to cloak its existence and its intention. Laws that violate our faith beliefs are a direct form of persecution.

To be a Catholic is not to be a member of a club that meets every Sunday. In order to be truly free to exercise our faith is to be unfettered to live our faith at every moment of every day. Religious freedom permits—even obligates—one to live his or her faith inside *and* outside of the church building.

Together let us celebrate the fact that Jesus Christ remains among us, for he wishes all of us to go to heaven and has provided us with guardian angels to look over us. May our nation and its government preserve our religious freedom so that we may freely exercise Jesus' invitation to "come and follow me." How may our younger brothers and sisters follow Jesus? Pope Francis has instructed that we should take to heart the following Beatitudes: "Blessed are the poor in spirit, for theirs is the kingdom of heaven. . . . Blessed are the merciful, for they will receive mercy. Blessed are the pure in heart, for they shall see God." (Mt 5:3, 7–8).

From your experience, is the Catholic Church playing a greater role in local people's lives?

This is a very good question as we live in the era of the New

Evangelization. However, it is a difficult question to answer because we are looking at different times in which the Church has been present. For example, there is a significant contrast between the Church in 1955 and the Church today.

In 1955, the Church was much more part of people's daily lives, from Sunday Mass attendance to parish-sponsored sports programs. Also, a larger percentage of Catholic youth attended Catholic schools. Not to mention, more men and women married in the Church and therefore established a spiritual foundation to their marriage. Still, there was a need for further growth and outreach, as Pope St. John XXIII indicated there was need for a New Pentecost.

Today, we are in the midst of the New Evangelization as begun by Pope St. John Paul II. St. John Paul insightfully acknowledged that the Church can do a better job at reaching out to Catholics, especially those who have fallen away from their faith. While I believe we are doing a better job at reaching out to Catholics, we have a long way to go in order to equip the laity in sharing the Faith with others. More forms of communication are at our disposal for evangelizing, especially as Catholic school enrollment has declined and as more Catholics have demonstrated the fact they need a refresher course on the definition of marriage. As you can see, the culture of the time impacts the manner in which the Church plays a role in people's lives. The answer is, unfortunately, yes and no.

Why do the Catholic bishops of the United States not endorse a presidential candidate?

While many organizations endorse publicly various candidates and initiatives in an election year, and are free to do so, the Catholic Church maintains the position that she has the teaching authority to educate the general population regarding the issues and how they directly affect our Catholic faith.

For instance, the Catholic bishops in the United States do not intend to tell Catholics for whom to vote, but instead help Catholics to form their consciences in accord with God's Truth. While the responsibility to make choices in political life rests with each individual voter, the teaching authority of the Church is to bring to light the truth for a properly formed conscience.

Many issues surround the present political arena and several should be taken seriously and guide an individual voter's conscience:

- respect for the lives of unborn children;
- respect for people who are terminally ill;
- protecting traditional marriage;
- avoiding excessive consumption of material goods due to destruction of our natural resources;
- protecting fellow Christians and religious minorities throughout the world;
- protecting religious freedom and our freedom of conscience, as well as the freedom of the Church to serve;
- economic policies to assist the poor;
- fixing our immigration system;
- promoting peace in our communities and our world.

All of the factors above should assist one in the determination of his or her political responsibility, especially during any election season. The Church's obligation to participate in the moral fabric of society is essential, as we recognize our right to vote should not be limited to a human endeavor, but one in which we share the truth of Jesus Christ in political dialogue, especially when it comes to which future path we intend our nation to take. Our public practice reflects our personal beliefs.

How do you feel about the tension between Catholicism and Congress?

Of course, it is not natural to seek arguments and difficult discussions for the sake of tension. However, in order to enlighten or instruct our lawmakers, there are times we, as Catholics, must communicate directly with our nation's leaders. This is why I, as a bishop, must affirm our leaders when they do the right thing and call their decisions into question when they do not. We see from some Catholic politicians that they openly practice their Catholic faith in their office of leadership, whereas others fail to do so and, instead, set a poor example for all.

For instance, when a Catholic in office respects the life of an unborn child, he or she is practicing his or her faith. When they do not, they betray the unborn child and our very faith.

As fellow Americans, we should be grateful we enjoy the freedom to encourage or to confront our civic leaders. In many countries of this world, my taking to task our nation's leaders could be punished by time in prison, or worse.

Together let us pray that the United States of America allows religious freedom to continue, for it has been challenged in the past and no doubt will be challenged in the future.

If Jesus was on this Earth today, what do you think would be different about today's society?

I know that you are framing your question around the contrast between Jesus' walking the earth in human form two millennia ago and our carrying on the mission as his Church in the Body of Christ, but we also recall that Jesus remains with us as he had promised to his disciples, "and behold I am with you always, until the close of the age" (Mt 28:20).

Jesus' presence endures among us and also has provided us with the capacity to know his will and follow his commandments.

For instance, Jesus established St. Peter and St. Peter's successors as the rock upon which he builds his Church, telling us that that the fires of hell will never prevail against it (Mt 16:18). Jesus entrusted St. Peter with the keys of the kingdom, thereby giving St. Peter, as well as his successors, authority to speak on his behalf.

Pope Francis' words of encouragement and correction in our contemporary era communicate to us whether or not we are following the commands Jesus has entrusted to the Apostles. We recall that following Jesus' Suffering, death, and Resurrection, that we as faithful disciples had much to do to change a world that did not necessarily follow Jesus' teachings.

Jesus entered a fallen world when he became man and our work is before us to share the salvation he has given us.

How does the Church feel about genetic modification? Because I don't believe we should mess with how God makes kids, but it can allow scientists to cure diseases.

This question is very timely, for often people believe the Church is anti-science. In fact, faith and reason are not meant to be separated, but instead complement each other. While volumes of works continue to be published concerning our knowledge of the genetic code and when it is responsible to utilize that knowledge, I will provide you with the common denominator: the human person.

We respect the gift of the human body, for it has been given to us by God himself. The technology we possess can benefit the overall health of the body or enhance one's quality of life. Unfortunately, there are times when selfish intentions govern our actions, actions which can have dire consequences. For instance, we must avoid the mindset of creating "designer children," that is, choosing whether or not one will be a boy or girl, or have a preferred hair color or height. On the other hand, if we are able to remove a cancer or life-threatening illness in order for a child to live, we accomplish something laudable.

The gift of genetic knowledge presumes responsibility and not the reckless and reprehensible attitude of: "If we can do it, then it must be right." We, made in God's image and likeness, are better than that. Each child is a gift and we have the profound responsibility to assist that child, who also is made in God's image and likeness. Our knowledge of genetics is a resource which can be of profound benefit to those whose lives may be in danger or in need of a cure.

What is the white square that priests wear on their collar? What does it stand for?

Over the past two millennia we have witnessed firsthand the Church's missionary work to share the Good News of Jesus Christ with a world so desirous to hear Christ's gift of eternal hope. The manner by which we believers exercise this apostolic work is conditioned by the respective cultures and time periods in which the Lord has placed us.

The white square, or "tab collar," to which you refer finds its source in a series of wardrobe modifications over the centuries that may be traced back even to the middle of the first millennium of Christianity. Not unlike other religious communities, the clergy has differentiated itself through clerical attire in different eras and cultures. In the beginning, the clerical attire was much simpler and, of course, in our present time, we have a number of vestitures such as religious habits. The tab collar is related to the Roman collar, but is much more recent in its arrival on the vestiture scene. The tab collar identifies a cleric, such as deacons, priests, bishops, and cardinals. Men who have received candidacy, that is, formal acceptance by their bishop to prepare for ordination, may wear the collar at specific times.

As a believing community, we are fortunate to have a plethora of ways in which we identify ourselves as ministers and sharers of the eternal hope in Jesus Christ. May God continue to bless our clergy and consecrated men and women as they bear witness to their undying faith in Jesus Christ, as well as their selfless attitude to share his love in an ever-changing world.

What religious orders take a vow of poverty?

Poverty is one of the three evangelical counsels, the other two being chastity and obedience.

The vow of poverty is a constitutive element of consecrated life, signifying a detachment from worldly things and providing voluntary humility. The one who takes the vow of poverty directs the gaze of all people on the endless treasures of the kingdom of heaven. The vow of poverty frees a person from the distractions of this world and gives that person the ability to deepen his or her encounter with Jesus Christ, who was poor for our sake.

The detachment from worldly goods reminds us where our priorities lie as fellow Christians.

How do you know if God's calling you to be a nun or priest?

This is a good question. Contrary to what we may hear or read at times, all vocations in the Church are not established by a "divine lightning strike." Wouldn't that be easy?

No, we are meant to quietly discern, which requires prayer and reflection, over whether or not we are receiving an invitation to serve God and his Church. Our service to God and his Church is realized especially through several vocations given to us in Holy Orders and the consecrated life. I invite you all to keep your hearts open to the possibility of serving God and his Church through one of these vocations. Moreover, I encourage all parents and families to recognize that your home, also known as the domestic church, is a vocational nursery enabling our younger brothers and sisters to grow in God's grace, thereby providing them the opportunity to discern God's will.

Pray over your Christian vocation and ask Jesus to share with you ways in which you may better hear his invitation to you. Reading about the various religious vocations is helpful, as well as discussing them with individuals who have entered that particular Christian way of life. Remember, all vocations come at the invitation of Jesus himself.

Another way to strengthen your certainty of whether or not Jesus is inviting you to serve him in a Church vocation is to visit with your parish priest or a religious man or woman who can help you determine the sacred path upon which Jesus has called you. Discernment weekends at the seminary or open houses at religious residences such as friaries, monasteries, and convents are very helpful to experience the consecrated and religious way of life. We can strengthen the religious vocations in our Church through constant prayer, both individually and as a community.

Why does the Pope have so many clothes and vestments since so many people in the world are poor?

Often we can get the impression that the pope is a billionaire and has the finest of everything, when in fact the pope has very few worldly possessions. For one, you recognize his beautiful white cassock, which, of course, comes in one color (yes, that was meant to be humorous). As for other possessions, Pope Francis has a thirty-year-old car, a Renault with 186,000 miles on it (donated to him). This is not a very expensive car, but you may also notice that wherever Pope Francis travels he has a security detail. Being an international figure, it is necessary for there to be a security contingent with the Holy Father in order to keep him safe. It is unfortunate, but we know all too well that public figures can sometimes be in danger because of individuals with evil intentions.

Where the pope lives in the Vatican actually is a small apartment, and while he has his own set of offices, they are in no way comparable to the megacorporations and governmental offices of our day.

Nevertheless, your point is well made in that it seems that Pope Francis has many, many good things as portrayed by much of the media. In fact, Pope Francis has very few possessions and the gifts that he has received from others he recently auctioned off with the proceeds going to the poor.

Pope Francis demonstrates how you and I are to live our faith; namely, to live it in a simple way and not filling our daily lives with distractions that keep us away from Jesus. Perhaps each one of us could go through our material possessions, like clothes, and decide whether someone else might benefit better from that article of clothing or material object.

If parents should not have favorites among their children, why did God favor Mary among other women to be the Mother of Jesus?

We are taught that parents should be fair to their children. What we read in the Gospel of Luke is the angel Gabriel telling Mary that she has been favored by God. Mary's kinswoman, Elizabeth, says the same thing. What does this mean? Simply that Mary has been completely faithful to the Lord and has remained good and pure in God's eyes. Moreover, the biggest reason why Mary is "full of grace" is that she accepts the role of being the Mother of Jesus, that is, the Mother of God.

So, let's address this question from a different angle. After Mary says yes to the invitation by God through the angel Gabriel to be Jesus' mother, she receives the Holy Spirit and becomes pregnant with Jesus. Obviously, Mary has a special place in the human race, a higher place, because she is the Mother of God and as a result is also the first Christian.

We should model ourselves after her holiness, humility, and love for God. We should model ourselves after the Immaculate Heart of Mary. That is why we pray the "Hail Mary," knowing that Mary is full of grace and she has the ability to intercede for us on our behalf, all while pointing toward her Son Jesus, the Savior of the world. Let us also not forget that Mary, our Mother in Faith, was without original sin. We hold to the truth of the Immaculate Conception and that Mary was taken body and soul to heaven at the Assumption.

Is Mary always present since they say our prayers go through Mary to God and Jesus? If she is not, how do our prayers go through her?

We know that Mary is the Mother of God; she is the Mother of Jesus. Mary, while being without sin, is still one of us. Mary is, inarguably, the first Christian.

As we know the truth that Mary was assumed body and soul into heaven, the Solemnity on August 15 (which is a Holy Day of Obligation) reminds us that Mary also is the Queen of Heaven and Earth. To be the Queen of Earth, of course, means that what we do personally matters to her. In other words, Mary is always available to help us, if only we take the time to ask.

Think about this the next time you pray the Rosary or participate in another Marian devotion: Mary is intently listening to you and me, especially our needs. When we pray to Mary in reaching for Jesus we do not leave a "heavenly voice-mail message" to be answered at a later time. Our Mother in Faith, Mary, the Mother of God, hears our prayers in real time and answers our prayers in real time. How blessed we are to have such a loving and merciful mother.

What is your opinion on the Holy Father's acceptance of same-sex marriage and divorced individuals?

Thank you for this timely question, for there are certain individuals out in the public media who interpret our Holy Father's conversations in a particular way, sometimes correctly and sometimes incorrectly.

Our Holy Father, in discussing the issue of Catholics who are divorced, reminds us that they are individuals in need of God's grace as much as you and me. Pope Francis reminds us that we as a faith community must be able to embrace all members and even pay special attention to those who may be suffering in a particular way. The Holy Father has not in any way changed the Church's approach to the sanctity of marriage, but reminds each and every one of us to exercise a compassionate heart regardless of the person's state in life.

As for same-sex unions, again, the Holy Father reminds

us to exercise a compassionate heart toward those who support civil same-sex marriages. Time and time again, Pope Francis has underscored the fact that marriage is between one man and one woman and that Jesus Christ has made it so.

This being said, our Holy Father instructs that we must exercise a merciful heart toward all as Jesus did, even those who were not living in complete conformity with the faith. Our Holy Father stresses the indissoluble nature of marriage and that the marriage itself is between one man and one woman, but along the same vein reminds us that in the midst of these truths another truth must be embraced: compassion toward others.

As a bishop, what role do you play in Catholic education?

As a successor of the first Apostles, I do not just govern (administrate) and sanctify (offer blessing), I also have the responsibility to teach or share our faith with everyone. I do this in a number of ways, one of which is obviously to defend the Deposit of Faith. What does that mean? Think about it: when you deposit money in the bank you are doing so to keep it safe, so that it does not disappear or diminish. Of course, the investment of our faith has eternal consequences and is much greater than any material goods we have here on Earth.

I also share our faith with others through both my words and my actions. You see, the Creed that we profess every Sunday is not just a collection of words that a bunch of people in our Church came up with over fifteen centuries ago. No, what we proclaim we are meant to live. In doing so, I as a teacher am sort of a "spiritual enabler" in that I help people to further delve into their faith. Our faith is not simply a bunch of dos and don'ts in a book and a bunch of prayers invented by a number of individuals over time. Rather, all of this of which I just spoke communicates the very relationship into which Our Lord Jesus Christ has invited us. In other words, all of our teaching centers on Jesus Christ.

Finally, and the one that tends to get bishops the most press, is when we have to stand up for the faith in times when it is not culturally or socially popular. That is the time when we have our integrity and courage tested. As a teacher, I constantly encourage all to reach out to the defenseless, such as our pre-born brothers and sisters as well as those in the final days of their life. Their dignity of life is no less than yours or mine and merits our protection. Also, we reach out to our brothers and sisters who are poor; namely, those who have lost their jobs or are disenfranchised from or marginalized by our society. These brothers and sisters need our help in the form of our self-sacrifice of time, treasure, and talent. You may read in the media that there are other areas where the bishop, as teacher, will "take a hit" by people who do not just disagree with the Church's teachings but lower themselves to insult and/or vindictiveness. Of course, none of us can take ourselves to that level, for it is Our Lord Jesus who has reminded us to be patient, as well as courageous, just as the saints before us in challenging times.

I am honored to be your bishop, and I joyfully embrace the task of teacher. How can one not be delighted to assist the growth of our Church in the faith handed over to us by the Son of God, Jesus Christ himself?

PRAYER

When Jesus is on the Cross he says, "My God, My God, why have you forsaken me?" Why does he say this? What does this mean?

The shortest and easiest answer is: Jesus died for us. This means that Jesus united with us in a very specific way. By not sinning, he took on all our own weaknesses and bore on his shoulders all of our sins. By saying these words which begin Psalm 22, he has united himself with us so that you and I can be reconciled to God. If you read on in Psalm 22, you realize that the psalm ends in very good news, for God will never leave us. It has been said also in ancient times that in order to refer to an entire psalm, someone would mention the first few words of that psalm and then people would understand the entire meaning of what he said. Here, Jesus is reminding you and me that his dying on the Cross is the greatest news of all for our salvation.

You may want to review Psalm 22 more thoroughly during Holy Week. As I have mentioned before, we must remember that the Bible is the story of our salvation. In other words, the stories and the passages in the Bible are about us.

How come Jesus prayed to God, if he is God?

Jesus often prayed to his Father in heaven, as indicated in the Gospel narratives. These moments of prayer are lessons to us all.

Firstly, Jesus indicates to us that he is the Son of God and speaks directly to God the Father. Different moments in his life on Earth, chronicled in the Gospel stories, indicate to us that Jesus was in constant contact with God the Father, doing the will of the Father, which was the Son's will, too.

Secondly, through his prayer to God the Father, Jesus instructs us that we, also, have the ability to speak with God through prayer. A great saint, St. John Damascene, once said, "Prayer is the raising of one's mind and heart to God or the requesting of good things from God" (see CCC 2559). In his prayer to God the Father, Jesus demonstrates how we should pray: with an open mind and heart to God's will.

Jesus shows us firsthand how we should be grateful that God listens to all of our prayers, even if sometimes his answer is no. Remember, in prayer, we do not bend God's will to ours, but instead allow God to bend our will to his.

How can we hear Jesus' voice when we are praying if we really can't hear it?

When Jesus speaks to us, he frequently speaks to us from within; we refer to that as Jesus speaking to our heart. We hear him best when we are free of distractions. When we let go of our own expectations and don't attempt to put words in God's mouth, we allow him to speak. This type of prayer is very difficult, for we are prone to have thoughts and images going through our minds. Still, when praying with the Bible or reciting a prayer from the treasury of prayers of the Church, we recognize Jesus' voice in the words, even if we recite them silently. Yes, Jesus speaks to us from the Bible and his words resonate within even if no external sound is made. Hearing Jesus is not limited to our ears.

On the other hand, we do hear Jesus when the Gospel is proclaimed at church, and during the Eucharistic Prayer as the bread and wine undergo transubstantiation into Jesus' Body and Blood. Jesus is speaking to us at the celebration of Mass each and every time. So, we *can* hear Jesus' voice—it comes in countless tones, accents, and languages.

How do you know if God is actually talking to you? Also, what is the best way to pray?

We all are aware that God wants us to talk to him. The greatest challenge is whether or not you and I are willing to listen. As human beings, we are prone to hear only what we want to hear, not necessarily what we need to hear. This can be so true in prayer, where we are invited to bend our will to God's will. Prayer is that conversation with God.

This being said, it is important that we speak with others in order to confirm whether or not God is actually talking to us. Hearing voices does not necessarily constitute that we are communicating with God, or the saints. God's voice is meant to go all the way into our inner being, not simply only to our senses.

I suggest you speak with your parents if you believe that the Lord is speaking to you, for regardless of our age, he brings us comfort and solace in a world that at times can be quite challenging. Remember, God will never leave you and he wants you to hear his voice. In addition to prayer, such as at Eucharistic Adoration, you can also hear his voice in the Bible readings, as well as in a number of ways at Mass. Think about it, every time you and I receive Jesus in the Eucharist, he is speaking to us, informing us that when we receive him we become more like him. Jesus constantly is inviting us into his friendship.

When I pray, does God understand when I get distracted?

As the saying goes, "God knows us better than we know ourselves." It seems to me that God does understand when we get distracted at prayer, but he does not encourage distraction. Prayer is conversation with God, so you and I do not want to inform God that we do not want to hear him, of course. We do, however, know that our minds can wander from time to time. Yes, this even happens to bishops. I am not proud to say that, but it shows that we need to work harder at listening to God.

Prayer is work. We must be able to clear our minds of worldly concerns so that we may hear from the One who created this world in which we live. We are fortunate to have so many forms of prayer, such as reading, speaking, meditating, or even contemplating (trying to keep very still and quiet— probably the most difficult form of prayer). In the material world, we get much of the information we need almost instantaneously by way of electronic media. God has all the information we need but he also wants us to be present to him, not just coming to him when we need favors.

Prayer is relationship. God wants to draw us closer to him. The closer we are to him, the better we can hear him. You and I can do our part by trying to put all distractions away while we pray. Those concerns will still be there when our prayer is completed.

Thank you for asking this question, for it does not seem like anyone is immune to distraction while at prayer. We just have to look more intensely at Our Lord Jesus, whose birth at Bethlehem over twenty centuries ago was God's announcement that he loves us more than we can imagine.

Why is the Rosary such a powerful weapon?

Did you know that the word "rosary" actually got its name from flowers? In fact, the word "rosary" comes from the Latin for a garland of roses. You mention that the Rosary can be a powerful weapon. This specific devotion to Mary is, of course, prayer, and prayer is definitely an extremely powerful weapon against evil.

In the Rosary, we pray for the intercession of Our Lady in our everyday life. In the midst of her assistance, we also pray the Apostolic Creed, as well as the Lord's Prayer, the Hail Mary, the Glory Be, the Fatima Prayer ("O My Jesus . . ."), and Hail Holy Queen, as well as the concluding prayer. The Rosary is a rich prayer devotion in the vast treasury of prayers in our Church. How blessed we are to have the Mother of God intercede for us as we live our lives as fellow Christian pilgrims.

Is it a sin to not pray every day?

God created each one of us in his image and likeness. However, this does not mean that we know everything God knows, or if what we are doing is actually right all of the time. We know that all of us are capable of doing exactly what God does not want us to do. We sin. Sin is a "deliberate thought, word, deed or omission contrary to the eternal law of God" (CCC, glossary).

It seems to me we need to ask the question: why do we not pray every day? Have we relegated our relationship with God to a secondary status beneath our own will and desire? Is it our intention to avoid God? Or, have we fallen into a bad habit of avoiding God?

Not praying to God may be the consequence of us sinning. Maybe we have done something wrong and we think that God will not listen to us because we crossed him. Perhaps not praying each day is our way of telling God that we do not need him. These are just questions, of course, but they are worth asking. Moreover, I, as a member of the clergy, have made a promise to pray every day and for me to break that promise is a sin.

I do not pray every day in order to avoid sin. It is in prayer that I can discern Jesus Christ's will for me and the work I must do as your shepherd. I pray in order to give God the glory he deserves from me and to further elevate myself to his enduring love.

When we are dedicating prayers for someone, should we be focusing on them or God in our heads while praying?

I apologize for my sense of humor, but the answer is: yes. When you and I pray, we are in a sense gazing on the face of God, even if we cannot see him with our own eyes. Nevertheless, we remember that prayer is raising our minds and hearts to God; in other words, prayer is conversation with God.

It is only natural that when we are offering prayers to God, such as for a family member or a friend in need, we picture that person's face. It seems to me this is very appropriate, as we share that image of the person for whom we are praying with Jesus himself. We are sharing with a friend in Jesus another friend who is in need of Jesus' mercy and love.

I hope this does not appear too complicated to understand. Remember, when we pray to God we are not leaving God a voicemail, text message, or tweet. We are in conversation with God in real time. Yes, really.

Even if you are not baptized, does God still answer your prayer?

God created all of us in his own image out of love. God the Son, Jesus Christ, has given us the great gift of Baptism, in which original sin is destroyed and we become more like Jesus with all the additional graces from the sacrament. This Sacrament of Initiation enables us to become a member of the Church's family.

We also are aware that while just over a billion of the

world's population is Catholic, most of our brothers and sisters in this world have not even been baptized. Each one of us is precious in God's eyes. The Gospel stories are full of Jesus' welcoming others and even blessing them. Jesus heard and answered the prayers of others, not just those of his closest friends. Jesus wants to be known by everyone.

These Gospel stories tell us that yes, if a non-baptized person prayed to God, he would hear their prayer. In fact, this would be a perfect time for the prayer to be answered by God. This moment of conversation with God may be the beginning of that person's journey to Baptism and his or her life in the Church. In prayer, God draws us closer to him, so that we can know him and love him as he loves us.

If two people get together and God is in their presence, then why would we pray the prayer again tomorrow?

You are probably referring to the words of Jesus when he says, "For where two or three are gathered in my name, there am I in the midst of them" (Mt 18:20). How grateful we are that Jesus is in our presence when we come together in prayer. We must remember, of course, that Jesus remains with us always. Therefore, praying to Jesus is not simply like calling him on the phone and hanging up when we're done. Jesus remains.

Each day, and hopefully, frequently, we should take time in prayer and conversation with Jesus. He has much to share with us, if only we are willing to listen. And, as you point out, how important it is that we are able to share Our Lord with others in prayer as well.

You and I can be fellow missionaries to the world by living our faith and demonstrating to others God's enduring presence among us.

Much is said in the New Evangelization within our own culture regarding our helping others to "rediscover" Jesus. We can also reach out to others to help them encounter Jesus again, even if they may come from a Christian family. We can keep each other in prayer and share with others the Good News of Jesus Christ by being kind, loving, and caring.

What are some ways Catholics can talk to God even when it is hard to?

Prayer is critical in our relationship with God. We should begin each day with a prayer of thanksgiving for the gift of the day and a prayer of intercession that each one of us may do God's will. Prayer is conversation with God. We also have the sublime gifts of the seven sacraments. Want to talk to God? Go to Confession. That is, speak to Jesus Christ acting through the priest in the confessional.

Also, every time we go to church we talk to God. Certainly, there are times when you and I may attend the Sacrifice of the Mass and be easily distracted. Yes, it can be difficult to train our attention on what is happening at Mass from beginning to end. Still, try. Never give up on trying to talk to God, for God never gives up on us.

When we pray to God, what should we focus on?

When we pray to God we are in conversation with God. This is true even at times when we feel it is a one-sided conversation; that is, we don't seem to hear God's voice. Never forget that God hears all of our prayers. So, as you pray, picture yourself speaking directly to the face of God. For instance, Jesus Christ taught us the Lord's Prayer (the Our Father), and so we should recognize that we are speaking to God the Father himself. Jesus also reminds us the great value each one of us has in God's eyes.

When you and I pray to God, we should focus on the face of God and not permit other things on the outside to distract us. How blessed we are that, made in God's image and likeness and through the great gift of Jesus' Incarnation and Paschal Mystery, we can be called children of God and address God as Father.

Why do people pray to Mary and the saints? Isn't that idolatry?

This is a good question, since many of our non-Catholic brothers and sisters, perhaps even some of our Catholic ones as well, mistake our *devotion* to the saints as *worship* of the saints. Of course, idolatry is worshipping something or someone as if it is a god. In our prayerful devotion to the saints we honor the saints, all the while worshipping Jesus Christ. Jesus is God and all saints point to him. Mary, the Mother of Jesus, takes us to him every time we pray the Hail Mary, the Rosary, or any other Marian devotion.

The members of the communion of saints—we mention

them in our Creed every Sunday—intercede with God on our behalf. The Catholic Church is not simply limited to the 1.2 billion Catholics who live among us. The Church includes those members who have died and gone before us. When we die, we do not lose our Catholic identity. We go to God as citizens of his heavenly kingdom. Yes, our heavenly citizenship surpasses our own national citizenship on Earth. While a country can remove or deny one's national identity, our baptismal gift is impossible to remove.

We pray to Mary and the saints, for all the saints are willing to assist us on our pilgrim's way. Life is a journey and we have heavenly guides, if only we take time to look. Isn't it great that we have "ultimate heroes" not just to imitate but to know with confidence they are there to help us? I encourage you to look up saints' names in Catholic resources to discover the treasure of divine help we are offered.

In the Bible, it says that we should not worship idols. When we genuflect to the statue of Mary or Jesus, is that bad?

We have within our tradition of the Church the use of statues as well as images of the saints for private and public devotion. What I mean by devotion is that we honor Mary, the Mother of Jesus, and all the saints, as well as pray for their intercession in our lives. Remember, the Catholic Church does not contain just all the Catholics here on Earth, but also the saints that are in heaven. They too are our brothers and sisters in the Catholic faith.

When we bow (genuflection is not necessary or required

in front of a statue or an image of a saint) or make a Sign of the Cross, we worship Jesus Christ through our honoring that saint. Remember, Mary, the Mother of God, has shown us the way to Jesus Christ, for she is the Mother of the Church. Her life here on Earth is a model for all Christians.

In honoring the saints through prayerful devotion and gesture, we do not worship any saint; we worship Jesus Christ the Son of God through our loving devotion to that saint.

I often worry about things out of my control, such as family member's safety while they travel. What Scripture passage would be good to read to remind me to trust God and what he has planned?

The uncertainty of this world can bring each one of us worry and anxiety. It's a good thing we have guardian angels to look over us and we can ask for the intercession of St. Christopher, patron saint of travelers, for protection. Your question had to do with the Bible, though.

Of all the passages in the Bible, the Lord's Prayer is the perfect travel companion. These words come directly from Jesus' mouth, and they instruct us how God always remains with us. When I say "travel," this also pertains to our pilgrimage or travel in this life. When we begin a car ride or our day with the Lord's Prayer, we can be confident that no matter what comes our way, God is right there.

The Book of Psalms and Book of Proverbs also provide numerous references to God's constant presence with us, here are some of my favorites:

- "I will instruct you and teach you in the way you should go; I will counsel you with my eye upon you." (Ps 32:8)
- "For he will give his angels charge of you to guard you in all your ways." (Ps 91:11)
- "Trust in the LORD with all your heart, and do not rely on your own insight. In all your ways acknowledge him, and he will make straight your paths." (Prov 3:5–6)
- "A man's mind plans his way, but the LORD directs his steps." (Prov 16:9)

St. Paul, in his Letter to the Philippians, reminds us that Jesus is always there, ready to give us whatever we need: "What you have learned and received and heard and seen in me, do; and the God of peace will be with you" (4:19). So, trust in God; he knows what he is doing, even if there are times we are unsure where we are going.

What saint do you pray to for surgery?

As one who has had surgery, I can personally say that I asked for more than one saint to intercede for a successful outcome. Of course, I asked Mary, in the Hail Mary, for her intercession, but there also were others. I have great admiration for St. Thérèse of Lisieux, and I asked for her prayers. St. John of God (born at the end of the fifteenth century) and St. Camillus (born the same year that St. John of God died, 1550) are patron saints of the sick. There also are patron saints for people suffering from specific ailments.

How about the surgeons? We have St. Luke (yes, one of the four evangelists) who is the patron saint of surgeons. We can certainly pray to St. Luke to assist the surgeon or surgical team who is preparing to help us.

Never forget we have a host of friends in heaven willing to assist us here on Earth (and those on the International Space Station) if only we are willing to ask for our saints' prayerful assistance. You and I mention in the Creed each week that we believe in the communion of saints. In other words, you and I are never alone. Never.

How many times do you pray in a day?

Of course I pray every day—I actually begin my day with a holy hour, and unless I have one scheduled later in the day, I also begin the day with the celebration of the Sacrifice of the Mass. When I was preparing for the priesthood in seminary formation, I was taught the Liturgy of the Hours, which consists of five sets of prayers said throughout the day. At my ordination to the diaconate, I promised to pray this Liturgy of the Hours, also known as the Breviary, each day. In doing so, I pray with the universal church.

In addition to these prayers, I also pray a Rosary and other prayerful devotions, depending on the circumstance. I am most grateful to pray in communities, and these prayers can be a simple prayer when visiting a home or a classroom. I even begin my day after waking up with a prayer thanking God for the day and asking for his blessings. May we all remember that in prayer, we do not bend to God's will to do our bidding, but instead bend our will to do God's will.

What is your favorite prayer?

For me, this is a very difficult question to answer because frequently I choose a prayer that already has a predetermined purpose. One of the very first prayers that I memorized as a child would most certainly be one of my favorite prayers, namely, the Lord's Prayer (or the Our Father). It is one of my favorites because Jesus shared it with us. The Lord's Prayer has been described by the Fathers of the Church as a fifty-five-word catechism. By that they mean that the richness of the words in this prayer cannot be exhausted. Even the first word in the prayer can teach us something: "our" is not "my." This pronoun itself shows us that we are members of a broader family of faith, and that we all share the same heavenly Father because Jesus has made it so through his Passion, death, and Resurrection.

This prayer helps us remember that we are a family focused on doing Jesus' work, which means bringing the kingdom of God here to Earth. Also, in praying this prayer with non-Catholics, I am repeatedly in awe of how many people actually have memorized this prayer. This shows another common element that connects all Christian churches, as we keep our gaze on Jesus Christ.